Accession no.
36165941

KU-302-515

In the last ten years or so an interest in musical authenticity has reached a wide
public. Many of the best-selling records of Bach, Handel, Haydn and Mozart are
those in which period techniques and period instruments are used. There is, however,
a danger that new 'authentic' dogmas of style and interpretation will come to replace
the anachronistic dogmas of the late romantic tradition. 'The search for an
"authentic" interpretation', writes Peter le Huray in his opening chapter, 'is not the
search for a single hard and fast answer, but for a range of possibilities from which to
make performing decisions.'

   This book introduces the performer to the problems that must be faced when
preparing an 'authentic' interpretation. It does so by focusing on nine representative
and well-known works from the baroque and classical periods, defining some of the
more important questions that the performer and listener should ask and suggesting
fruitful lines of enquiry.

   It is essential reading and reference material for player, student and listener alike.

WITHDRAWN

Authenticity in performance

Fig. II.<sup>da</sup>

From *A Treatise on the Fundamental Principles of Violin Playing* by Leopold Mozart

# AUTHENTICITY IN PERFORMANCE

## EIGHTEENTH-CENTURY CASE STUDIES

PETER LE HURAY

*Fellow of St Catharine's College, Cambridge*
*and University Lecturer in Music*

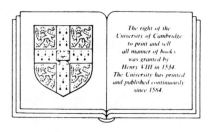

LIS LIBRARY

| Date | Fund |
|------|------|
| 05/10/12 | d-che |

Order No
2347969

University of Chester

The right of the
University of Cambridge
to print and sell
all manner of books
was granted by
Henry VIII in 1534.
The University has printed
and published continuously
since 1584.

CAMBRIDGE UNIVERSITY PRESS

*Cambridge*

*New York*   *Port Chester*

*Melbourne*   *Sydney*

CAMBRIDGE UNIVERSITY PRESS
Cambridge, New York, Melbourne, Madrid, Cape Town, Singapore, São Paulo, Delhi

Cambridge University Press
The Edinburgh Building, Cambridge CB2 8RU, UK

Published in the United States of America by Cambridge University Press, New York

www.cambridge.org
Information on this title: www.cambridge.org/9780521399265

© Cambridge University Press 1990

This publication is in copyright. Subject to statutory exception
and to the provisions of relevant collective licensing agreements,
no reproduction of any part may take place without the written
permission of Cambridge University Press.

First published 1990
Re-issued in this digitally printed version 2009

*A catalogue record for this publication is available from the British Library*

*Library of Congress Cataloguing in Publication data*

Le Huray, Peter.
    Authenticity in performance: eighteenth-century case studies
    Peter le Huray.
        p.    C.
    ISBN 0 521 39044 3. ISBN 0 521 39926 2. (pbk.)
    1. Performance practice (Music) – 18th century.   I. Title.
ML457.L4   1990
781´4´3´09033–dc20                            89–70827 CIP
                                              MN

ISBN 978-0-521-39044-6 hardback
ISBN 978-0-521-39926-5 paperback

To Bridget

# Contents

# Music examples

# Preface

Interest in rediscovering earlier styles of performance is no recent development. Arnold Dolmetsch's *The Interpretation of the Music of the XVII and XVIII Centuries* (London, 1915; revised 1944) contains the fruit of half a century's experience of 'early' music, in the fields of performance, instrument-making and musical scholarship. Only recently however has an interest in 'authenticity' reached out to a wide musical public. Many of the best-selling records of Bach, Handel, Haydn and Mozart are now those in which 'period' instruments and 'period' techniques are used. Much that is now published about baroque and classical music is to do with performance. Performance research has never been more intense at all levels than it now is, and the fields of enquiry are steadily widening.

There is however a danger that new 'authentic' dogmas of style and interpretation will come to replace the anachronistic dogmas of a late Romantic tradition, the shortcomings of which are now increasingly realised by informed professionals and an informed musical public. This little book does not aim nor could it ever hope to offer a set of 'right' answers. Performance, after all, is a recreative act in which the imagination of the performer plays a vital role. The objectives of this book, rather, are to define some of the more important *questions* that the performer and listener should ask, to suggest fruitful lines of enquiry, and in doing so to supply, as far as is humanly possible, references to the most informed and up-to-date information that is currently available.

It would have been possible to arrange the following pages in quite a different way, taking – one by one – the major issues: 'source' problems; instrumental sonorities; performance techniques; notational conventions such as 'inequality', overdotting, tempi, dynamics and ornamentation; and especially such interpretative issues as articulation and phrasing. Though an arrangement of this kind might have the superficial attraction of simplicity and orderliness, it would carry with it the temptation to overgeneralise, to ignore the fact that performance conventions were subject to constant change, that they undoubtedly differed from place to place, and even from composer to composer. Instead of following a subject-by-subject format, therefore, the book is organised into discussions of selected compositions, each representing a major genre of its time. In all but one case a facsimile of either the first edition or autograph is readily available, and all are accessible in good modern editions. The aim has been not only to define the perform-ance conventions that apply to each work, but also to relate each discussion as closely as possible to the actual processes of making music: to go through the stages, in other words, that any thinking musician might choose to follow when preparing a work for performance. It is hoped, nonetheless, that the subject index (p. 201) may serve as a useful guide to the specific issues that are addressed during the course of the book.

The danger of the present format is that it may encourage a compartmen-talised approach to interpretation. Although the second chapter, for inst-ance, is concerned with a work for keyboard, there is much in it that is of general relevance to all instrumental music of the period. Similarly, there is much in the subsequent chapter on string playing that will help the keyboard player to grasp principles of baroque articulation. There should be no artificial boundaries between instruments or genres in any genuine discus-sion of performance practice.

Performance practice (to use that ugly but convenient term) is a con-tinuing subject of enquiry. Almost every month new ideas on 'authentic' performance are being published and new 'authentic' performances re-corded. If this brief study serves to open out fresh approaches, if too it succeeds in demonstrating, not only to the performer but to the listener and to the student, the relevance of such 'peripheral' disciplines as analysis and text criticism, then it will have served its purpose.

# Acknowledgements

Of the many friends who have at one time or another offered invaluable help and encouragement I cannot fail to mention Professor Peter Aston, Dr John Butt, Dr Glyn Jenkins, Dr Andrew Jones, Dr David Jones, Mrs Marie Leonhardt-Amsler, Mrs Virginia Pleasants, Mr Anthony Rowland-Jones, and Professor Michael Talbot. A particular thank you is due to Professors Howard Brown, Robin Stowell and Peter Williams, who, during the later stages of the work, devoted much time and thought to improving both its form and content. I am most grateful, too, to Richard Andrewes, Curator of the Cambridge University Music Faculty Library, and to Mrs Cranmer, librarian of the Rowe Music Library, King's College, for their generous assistance, as also to Penny Souster of Cambridge University Press, and Kathryn Bailey, whose editorial skills have made the book infinitely more readable. Acknowledgement is due, too, to Dr Philip Hazel, whose elegant music-setting programme I have used for many of the music examples.

# I

## The spirit of authenticity

Vaughan Williams once compared a page of music to a railway timetable. The page, he said, tells us no more about the living experience of the music than the timetable tells us about the sights to be enjoyed during the journey. The truth of this typically challenging remark has never been more widely accepted than it is today. Never before has there been such concern to reach beyond the musical notation in the search for lost traditions of performance. Not long ago, many eminent musicians simply assumed with breathtaking self-assurance that composers of earlier times would have preferred to hear their music played by modern ensembles, on modern instruments, and in the modern manner, rather than on the 'imperfect' instruments of their own times. To be sure, Arnold Dolmetsch was reviving early instruments and studying how they should be played as long ago as 1885.[1] Only during the last twenty years or so, however, have significant numbers of professional musicians begun to interest themselves in such matters, taking their ideas into the concert hall and the recording studio for a large but uninitiated public to enjoy. August Wenzinger's *Schola Cantorum Basiliensis* was one of the first 'authentic' groups to attract widespread attention, notably through the recordings that it made for DGG in the 1950s. Ten or so years later the pace of change accelerated. To begin with, J. S. Bach was the focus of attention. Nikolaus Harnoncourt's *Concentus Musicus* made history with their Telefunken Brandenburgs (1964). Shortly afterwards, in association with the Leonhardt Consort, they embarked on a truly colossal undertaking – a complete recording of the Bach cantatas. More recently, 'authentic' groups have been spreading their nets ever more widely, both backwards and forwards from 1700. Monteverdi's *Vespers* has been one of the greatest popular successes of the 'early music' revival, whilst in the classical field, 'authentic' performances of Haydn, Mozart and Beethoven are well represented in the gramophone catalogues. Certainly there is now no lack of opportunity to hear how professional musicians are trying to penetrate beyond the 'railway timetable' to the original musical experience.

But is perhaps the present interest in 'authenticity' simply a reflection of a lack of professional self-confidence? Why all this concern to discover how the music may have sounded at the time of its composition? Is not music a performing art, in which the recreator has just as much right to an opinion as the creator? No one is suggesting, surely, that the time will ever come when Beethoven's piano sonatas will be played *only* on early nineteenth-century Viennese instruments, or that pianists will be banned from playing the '48', on the grounds that Bach wrote the preludes and fugues for clavichord, harpsichord and chamber organ – his 'well-tempered' keyboards! And what if the composer did give precise instructions as to speed, dynamics, articulation and instrumentation? Surely the performer must be the ultimate judge? The early nineteenth-century pianist and historian, Lenz, tells of a visit to young Liszt in Paris in the early 1830s.[2] Lenz was hoping for some lessons, and had taken along a Weber piano sonata to play. Liszt, obviously very bored at the thought of yet another pupil, beckoned him to a piano. As Lenz proceeded, however, Liszt sat up and was soon at the keyboard, sight-reading the music for himself. He ran the A flat major Sonata through, trying passages now fast, now slow, now loud, now soft, regardless of the composer's instructions, asking Lenz which he preferred. Here then surely is ample precedent for a freely creative approach to interpretation?

Closer investigation of early Romantic attitudes to interpretation, however, reveals a very different spirit at work amongst many musicians. The impulsive and self-willed Berlioz, for example, felt passionately that music should not be tampered with. In his *A Travers Chants* (Paris, 1862) he strongly condemned the practice of reorchestrating established masterpieces, tracing this back to Mozart, whose wind parts to *Messiah* are still commonly used. 'Even the greatest symphonist the world has ever seen has not escaped this indescribable kind of outrage [he wrote] . . . and they have already begun to correct the instrumentation of the C MINOR SYMPHONY!'

The reorchestration of music is, of course, a gross example of a deliberate disregard for the composer's intentions. Disregard, however, manifests itself more commonly at deeper levels of interpretation, and it is a disregard (significantly enough) that several leading twentieth-century composers have intensely resented. In his 1939 Norton lectures at Harvard, for instance, Stravinsky went so far as to suggest that performance is an ethical matter – a question so to speak of musical 'morality':

> The sin against the spirit of a work [he wrote] always begins with a sin against its letter and leads to . . . endless follies . . . Thus it follows that a *crescendo* . . . is always accompanied by a speeding up of movement, while a slowing down never fails to accompany a *diminuendo*. The superfluous is refined upon; a *piano*, *piano pianissimo* is delicately sought after; great pride is taken in perfecting useless nuances – a concern that usually goes hand in hand with inaccurate rhythm.[3]

Many echoes of Stravinsky's ideas on performance are to be found in Hindemith's Harvard lectures, which he delivered there six years later. He particularly deplored the exaggerated role accorded to the performer. As he put it:

> This high evaluation of the intermediate transformer station between the generator of a composition and the consumer . . . is dangerous – It seduces the listener to slide down 'irresistibly' until the lowest point of perception is reached, when nothing else counts but the performer's virtuosity, the pleasant-sounding emptiness, the uninhibited superficiality.[4]

Arnold Schoenberg tended to take a more sophisticated and at the same time more optimistic view of the performer of his day than did either Hindemith or Stravinsky. Like Vaughan Williams, he was particularly conscious of the inadequacies of the printed page. And yet he, too, was in no doubt that the composer's wishes, as far as they could be determined, should be respected:

> It must be admitted [he wrote] that in the period around 1900 many artists overdid themselves in exhibiting the power of the emotion they were capable of feeling; artists who believed themselves to be more important than the work – or at least than the composer.[5]

Olivier Messiaen also is keenly aware of the limitations of conventional score notation, but he too, argues that good performance demands the closest attention to what the composer has written.[6] To be sure, composers have from time to time built into their music techniques that give the performer some freedom in the choice of speeds, rhythms and dynamics. In some modern compositions the performer is even invited to choose where to begin and end the piece, and which pitches and rhythms to play. Normally, however, the composer expects the performer to begin at the beginning and end at the end, and to follow all the instructions in the score in chronological order.

If, then, composers tend to mean what they write, it is our duty as performers to try to find out as much as possible about that meaning. It is as much a question of ethics as aesthetics. This is not for a moment to suggest, however, that musical 'meaning' has a fixed and absolute value – that there can be only *one* way of playing a particular piece. For as Vaughan Williams aptly put it:

> a musical score is merely an indication of potential music . . . . a most clumsy and ill-devised indication. How clumsy it is may be seen from the importance of the 'individual renderings' of any piece of music. If a composer could indicate what he wanted with any precision there would be no room for this; as it is, two singers or players may follow faithfully the composer's intentions as given in the written notes, and yet produce widely differing results.[7]

He might well have gone on at that point to say that this is one of the particular joys that music shares with the other performing arts: that a musical object can be viewed from many different angles and yet remain essentially the same piece.

The search for an 'authentic' interpretation, therefore, is not the search for a single hard and fast answer, but for a range of possibilities from which to make performing decisions. The age of the music will determine what kinds of search the performer has to make. Whatever its age, the composition will need to be analysed closely to see what its overall structure is, what its musical themes or motives are, and how these are developed, phrase by phrase, to create a vital and coherent whole. The analytical process will, of course, involve insights of differing kinds, according to the type of music being investigated, and its time and place of origin. The impact of Bach's Fifth Brandenburg Concerto, after all, is far removed from that of Beethoven's 'Emperor' Concerto, and that of Beethoven's early F minor Piano Sonata from Debussy's *La Fille aux cheveux de lin*.

Analysis apart, there are other avenues that the perceptive performer will wish to explore. In more recent times, composers themselves have been increasingly particular about the ways in which they would like their music to be played. Debussy, for instance, spoke of the aural ideal of a hammerless piano; Chopin wrote of his intense dislike of tub-thumping German pianism. The further back in time we go, however, the more sketchy is the evidence of this kind, the less informative is the musical notation itself, and the less familiar are the instruments and the techniques of playing them. Every avenue of enquiry must nonetheless be explored in the search for the fullest possible picture of the original, a picture that will more clearly define the range of choices that are open to the performer. The violinist who is learning one of Bach's unaccompanied sonatas or partitas, for instance, will doubtless be using a modern edition rather than a facsimile of the original. This will need to be checked against the readily accessible facsimile of Bach's autograph to ensure that every detail of the original has been clearly reproduced, and that every editorial adjustment and clarification is clearly visible as such. As much as possible should be discovered, too, about the type of violin that a player of Bach's day might have used – about its stringing and its 'soul' (the bow), and about the techniques of applying the bow to the strings. Not every question will find a ready answer, but until every potential source of information has been checked the player will be in no position to assess the strengths and weaknesses of modern techniques and interpretative approaches.

Authenticity is no dogma. There has never been, nor can there ever be, *one* way of interpreting a composition. Neither is it practicable or even desirable to insist exclusively on 'period' instruments and 'period' techniques. Humility must be a vital ingredient of the modern performer's equipment: the humility to read, to analyse and to listen, and the humility to modify accepted assumptions where necessary in order to transform the 'timetable' into a truly *musical* journey.

# Bach's C major Prelude BWV 870 and 870a

ON CHOOSING A GOOD EDITION

The very first thing to be done in preparing a performance is to ensure that the edition being used is up to date. No one would dream of using an out-of-date timetable to plan a journey; but how many musicians take the trouble to find out whether their 'timetable' – the edition from which they are working – is the current one? In what ways, though, can a musical score be 'out of date'? Surely, all the printer has to do is to reproduce exactly what the composer wrote? In an ideal world this would indeed be the case. Sadly, however, things are never quite as simple or straightforward as they may seem. Take the piano music of Chopin, for instance. Most of it was published during the composer's lifetime, and with the composer's approval. On the face of it, this would seem to be a perfect situation, for direct links can be established between the composer and the first printed editions of his music. There are, however, hidden and formidable snags. Chopin published much of his music in three different countries simultaneously – Germany, France and England – using three different publishers. To do this, he had three sets of copies made, and each publisher was sent a set from which were then produced the printed editions. Unfortunately, Chopin did not always check carefully the manuscript copies that he sent to the publishers, still less the printed editions that were made from them. As a result there are many differences of detail between the French, German and English editions, many of which are not simply obvious mistakes. One solution might be to ignore the printed editions and concentrate on the autographs. Many of these have been lost, however. To make matters more difficult, Chopin tended to go back to his earlier compositions from time to time to revise them. Some of the differences that are to be found in surviving copies of a piece, therefore, could be genuine 'second thoughts' rather than oversights and mistakes.

If difficulties of this size arise from such an apparently straightforward case, how much more formidable then are the problems that Beethoven's untidy scores create. And even these problems pale into insignificance beside those that arise in connection with much earlier music. The older the music, the poorer the sources tend to be. Before 1600, in particular, autographs and good quality publications are rare. Much early notation is inexact, and the older it is the less performance 'information' it will contain: phrasings, expression marks and speed indications, for example, are practically non-existent in pre-eighteenth-century music.

All these matters call for the attention of an expert editor: someone who knows the music of the period intimately, and who is familiar with its sources. His task will be to sift out the good sources from the bad, and to decide which version is to form the basis of his edition. Some of the decisions that he will have to make will be easy. A wrong note is usually obvious enough, as is a wrong time value. Accidentals, though, are not always clearly right or wrong, whilst variants of other kinds can be teasingly difficult to pin down.

No matter how carefully and skilfully the editor may have completed his task, his edition will be of little use to the performer unless he clearly explains to the reader what he has done to the original score, and why he has done it. To begin with, the edition should contain a brief description of the sources that have been used. If the editor has had to change or add to the original notation in any way, he should then explain the need for the changes and alterations and describe how the reader may see what has been done. If an accidental has had to be altered, for instance, it should look different from an original one – it could be shown in small type, for instance, or placed above rather than at the side of the note. Unless the edition clearly shows what the editor has done to the original, it should be either consigned to the waste-paper basket or carefully checked against an up-to-date edition (such as the Associated Board edition of Mozart's piano sonatas, edited by Stanley Sadie and Denis Matthews). Most nineteenth- and early twentieth-century editors carried out their work in an extraordinarily highhanded manner, as we shall shortly see, correcting 'errors' without a word of warning, and liberally covering the pages with slurs, dots and 'expression' marks of their own. In doing so, they often transformed the intended spirit of the original composition beyond recognition. Unfortunately, far too many misleading editions are still in print. More will be said later on in the book about editorial problems – especially in the chapter on Haydn's 'Drum Roll' Symphony (p. 149). These preliminary remarks, however, may serve as a general introduction to a vital yet much neglected aspect of performance.

How can a good edition of Bach's *Das wohltemperirte Clavier* (commonly translated as 'The Well-Tempered Clavier') be identified? To begin with, the performer has a right to know something about the original sources which the editor has used. Neither the first nor the second book of the '48' was published during Bach's lifetime, but by great good fortune Bach's own manuscripts have survived, together with copies made by a close circle of pupils and friends. The first problem that the editor must decide is whether to use only Bach's own copies (the primary sources, that is to say), or to look at secondary sources as well, particularly those that were copied out by Bach's pupils. It could be, for instance, that a copy in the hand of a Bach pupil contains second thoughts scribbled down by the composer during the course of a lesson. Bach's early editors tended to take the simple way out, selecting what seemed to be the most reliable source and publishing it with whatever emendations they felt were necessary. The 'New and Correct Edition' by S. Wesley and C. F. Horne (London c. 1830) is typical of its kind. The editors seem to have used the largely autograph copy of Book 1, though they say nothing about this in their lengthy preface (were they too inexperienced, perhaps, to know that they were working from the autograph?). They reproduced the original exactly as they found it, barring a minor slip here and there, and apart from the addition of half a dozen signs to indicate different types of fugal entry. Friedrich Chrysander's Wolfenbüttel edition of 1856 presents an equally clean text. It does, however, diverge in places from the autograph. The editor tells us nothing about the sources he used, nor indeed would he have known much (if anything) about the secondary copies, for it is only recently that scholars have managed to identify some of the handwritings of Bach's pupils and friends. All one can say of Chrysander's edition is that it does not follow Bach's autograph, and that no good reasons are given for the differences that arise. Moving on to Czerny's celebrated edition (Vienna 1838), we enter an altogether different world (see Example 3 below). 'Our chief aim [wrote Czerny] has been to make this *New Edition of John Sebastian Bach's 48 Preludes and 48 Fugues* as correct and perfect as possible; for this purpose we have compared together every previous edition, as well as several ancient manuscripts.' The mere act of comparison is valueless, however, unless the worth of what is being compared is known, a matter that Czerny delicately sidestepped. Little confidence can be placed in his judgement, for he makes no mention at all of the existence of an autograph! Czerny's brazen assurances of 'correctness' and 'perfectness', moreover, are totally contradicted by the appearance of the printed page: most of the actual notes are accurate enough, to be sure, but Czerny has added a whole battery of dynamic signs, from *pp* to *ff*, and the music is peppered with phrasings and staccato marks. From the preface, it is clear that Czerny had heard 'many of the Fugues played by the great *Beethoven*', and that his edition reflects that experience, rather than the 'correctness' and 'perfection' of Bach's originals. It will, therefore, be of greater interest to students of Beethoven than of Bach. Nevertheless, it was still being reprinted by the eminent firm of Peters more than a hundred years after it was first published, and it has perhaps been the most influential of all nineteenth-century editions. Czerny's misleading work is similar in spirit to the way in which Liszt arrogantly altered the speeds, phrasings and dynamic markings of Weber's piano music when he sight-read it to Lenz in 1830.

The editor's job, then, is to represent Bach's intentions as faithfully as possible. A good editor will, of course, try to help the performer with problems of interpretation but he will do this in such a way that there is no danger of confusing editorial suggestions with the composer's original notation. As has already been said, the older the music, the more numerous are the interpretative problems likely to be. Bach's autograph of the '48', for instance, tells us nothing about the type of instrument Bach had in mind, the sort of touch he would have used (how much legato and how much staccato, i.e. the articulation), the speed (or tempo) of the music and whether it is to be loud or soft (its dynamic levels). These are complex matters that cannot be ignored by the responsible editor, even if clear-cut answers are not always possible.

### FINGERING AS EVIDENCE OF PERFORMANCE STYLE

The addition of fingerings is an apparently innocent activity in which almost all Bach editors have indulged. Bach's gifted son, Carl Philipp Emanuel, made the point, in his *Versuch über die wahre Art das Clavier zu spielen* (Berlin, 1753),[1] that good performance depends upon well-chosen fingerings. He particularly stressed the part that his father had played in developing a fingering system suited to the new music of the day, in which extreme 'sharp' and 'flat' keys were increasingly common. Unfortunately, very little fingering is to be found in the early sources of Bach's keyboard music, and only one very minor example is in Bach's own hand. The modern editor, then, finds himself in a difficult position: he knows that the Bach family were taught systematic fingerings, and yet he has very little first-hand knowledge of that system. Before he suggests any fingerings he clearly has to learn as much as he can from those that survive, few as these may be. The question here is not simply one of keyboard technique but of interpretation, for as we shall see, fingerings can tell us a good deal about articulation – phrasing, legato and staccato.

The one piece that contains autograph fingerings is a little *Applicatio* or exercise that he wrote out for his young son Wilhelm Friedemann in 1720 when the boy was nine years old (see Example 1). The *Applicatio* is fully fingered, in a way that may surprise the modern pianist. Basically the piece is no more than a C major scale with a few chords added. The stepwise notes of the scale are to be played by paired fingerings, the strong third and first fingers being placed on the odd-numbered notes (i.e. the relatively accented ones). The principle of playing stepwise passages in this way had already

**Ex. 1**  J. S. Bach, *Applicatio* for Wilhelm Friedemann

been established by 1550. Bach's sixteenth-century predecessor at Leipzig, Elias Ammerbach, used a version of it in his *Orgel oder Instrument Tabulatur* of 1571 (2nd edn 1583). Interestingly, Bach owned a copy of this book (now in the University Library, Cambridge) and had studied it closely enough to write annotations in the margins. Certain scholars have leapt upon this piece of evidence to argue that paired fingerings must be the basis of 'authentic' Bach performance. Some have even claimed that the fingerings were naturally bound to produce paired phrasings, and even rhythmic unevenness, the odd notes being held longer than the even ones. Neither assumption can be proved, and, indeed, smooth, legato lines are perfectly possible with paired fingerings, provided that there are not too many sharps and flats. In any case the little *Applicatio* is comparatively unimportant for it is only a technical exercise, and an outdated one at that. It certainly does not represent the *new* system of fingering which C. P. E. Bach describes as having been developed by his father.

Fortunately a fingered early version of the C major Prelude and Fugue from the second book of the '48' has survived (Example 2). It is in the hand of one of Bach's pupils, Johann Caspar Vogler, and it is easily the most important remaining example of 'Bach' fingering.[2] The beginning of Czerny's edition of the Prelude is shown in facsimile in Example 3.

**Ex. 2**  J. S. Bach, Praeludium BWV 870a, with fingering

**Ex. 3** J. S. Bach, Praeludium BWV 870, edited by Czerny

There is no *proof* that Vogler's fingerings come from Bach. All that can be said about them is that the watermark of the paper is identical to one that is to be found on paper that Bach used. Whatever the origin, these fingerings do tell us much about the way that the C major would have been played by a Bach pupil. In the fourth bar of the Prelude, for example, Czerny (and most later editors) finger the left-hand part in such a way as to make possible a very smooth legato. Vogler's fingering, on the other hand, places the thumb successively on F, E, D and E. A slight break between each pair of notes is therefore inevitable. Interestingly, Czerny places the right thumb on B, as Vogler does, making a slight articulation between G and B unavoidable. He then places 2 on the succeeding C, in legato fashion, whereas Vogler lifts the thumb from B to C, again producing an unavoidable (if slight) articulation. A comparison of other points at which the two versions diverge reveals in each case that *legato* phrasings are more easily achieved with Czerny's fingerings. This is especially noticeable in upbeat to downbeat contexts: compare for instance right-hand fingerings in bars 4–5, 11–12 and 13 (beats 2–3), and left-hand ones in 6–7, 9 (beats 2–3) and 13–14. As far as ties are concerned, Vogler's fingerings suggest that the length of a tied pair was normally shortened to make room for a slight break before the following note. Czerny's fingerings, on the other hand, enable the tied notes to be held for their full values (compare the fingerings in bar 6 of the Prelude, for instance). Vogler's fingerings in the fugue are less informative, though again the conclusion must be that Vogler played in a more detached manner than Czerny would have done. This is particularly evident in the fingering of the second entry of the subject: Vogler places the second finger of the right hand on the upper E of bar 6, making some degree of detachment from the preceding G almost unavoidable. His fingerings in bars 13–17 confirm this, and suggest at least some separation of the two crotchets in the subject; Czerny, on the other hand, actually uses phrase marks to bind the two crotchets together. It is worth mentioning, in passing, that Vogler does not use finger substitution at all (i.e. the replacing of one finger by another on a sustained note to ensure a total legato). This technique seems first to have been introduced by François Couperin, but it was not extensively used until the early years of the nineteenth century.

## BACH'S KEYBOARD INSTRUMENTS

In an attempt to fill out some of the missing details of the musical 'timetable', we have already reached far beyond Bach's uninformative autograph score. But there are still many questions to ask before a performance can be attempted. The most obvious of these perhaps concerns the kind of instrument or instruments that Bach may have had in mind for the '48'. He seems here deliberately to have left the choice to the performer. His title, *Das wohltemperirte Clavier*, means no more and no less than the well-tuned keyboard. In Bach's day there were four main groups of keyboard instruments: those that plucked strings – principally, of course, harpsichords; those that struck strings with tangents – namely clavichords; those that struck strings with hammers – pianos; and those that blew pipes – organs. As far as pianos were concerned, Bach certainly admired Silbermann's new grand pianos when he visited Dresden in 1747 to see his son, Carl Philipp Emmanuel. This was some three or four years after he had completed the second book of the '48', however. Although with hindsight we might imagine such a piece as the E minor Prelude in Book 2 being written with the piano specially in mind, there is no concrete evidence to support or deny this. Undoubtedly, the harpsichord is appropriate for at least some of the '48'. The organ, too, cannot entirely be ruled out, though perhaps a small one-manual instrument without pedals, rather than a large church organ. Certain preludes and fugues do go particularly well on these instruments, without a doubt: the French overture style D major Fugue from Book 1 is ideally suited for the harpsichord, for instance, and the B flat major and B major Fugues from Book 2 for the organ. And yet, if just one instrument had to be chosen, it would surely be the clavichord, for though the clavichord might not sound as brilliant as the harpsichord in the A minor Fugue of Book 2, or as full as the organ in the B flat minor Fugue of Book 1, it is unrivalled for such reflective pieces as the E flat minor and B flat minor Preludes of Book 1, and the F sharp minor and A minor Preludes of Book 2. Although the harpsichord family of instruments was undoubtedly pre-eminent in France, Italy and England at the time, in Bach's Germany the clavichord was by far the most popular domestic keyboard instrument. And, as C. P. E. Bach observed, the clavichord revealed most clearly the musicianship of the keyboard player (C. P. E. Bach, *Versuch*, p. 36).

The clavichord differs from the organ and harpsichord in that variations of touch/weight directly affect the volume of the sound. In this respect it is much closer to the piano than to the other two instruments.[3] Clavichord dynamics, however, are a matter of subtle gradation rather than sheer volume, as indeed they are on the early piano. Eighteenth-century German builders were certainly managing to get more volume out of the clavichord; the simple fact remained, nonetheless, that if the player hit a note too hard, it was forced out of tune.[4] The clavichords of Bach's day may have been less 'expressive' than the modern piano in terms of dynamic *range*; their transparent, clearly articulated sounds, nonetheless, encouraged a performance style of great expressive subtlety.

## PHRASING AND ARTICULATION

This brings us back to the heart of the matter, for the notes of the C major Prelude would certainly not all have been played *exactly* as they appear on the page. The few fingerings that have already been examined are proof enough of that. But just how legato would Bach have played the piece? How strictly would he have kept to one speed? Might he have used any kind of rubato? And would he have thought in terms of long musical phrases? After all, extended phrase markings covering several bars only began to appear in music towards the end of the eighteenth century.

As we have already seen, Bach's own notation covers only the bare essentials of pitch and rhythm. No more than a handful of articulation marks (slurs and staccato dots and dashes) are to be found in Bach's own copy of the '48'. There are also a few extra marks in the copies that Bach's friends and pupils made. Even so, only fourteen of the forty-eight pieces are involved and many of the marks raise more questions than they answer.[5] The sighing, appoggiatura-like subject of the B minor Fugue, for instance, is phrased in paired quaver groups (Example 4a). The first two entries are fully phrased. The third entry is only partially phrased, whilst all the rest are unmarked. The manuscript source of the phrasing is a copy made by one of Bach's pupils. Perhaps then the phrasing was added during a lesson, in the way that C. P. E. Bach describes:

> There is an occasional convenience to be noted concerning pieces in which many accented or slurred notes follow each other in succession; this is that only the first ones are marked, it being understood that the markings continue until [the figuration] ceases.[6]

But what does the phrasing actually mean? Is it simply to bind pairs of quavers together, in which case, are all the other quavers to be played in a detached manner? Or is the duration of the first quaver to be longer than that of the second? Rather similar pairs of quavers crop up in the D major Prelude (bars 2, 4 and 44 – see Example 4b). In each case only one of two lines moving in parallel thirds or sixths is phrased. Are the non-phrased parallel parts to be played in a detached manner? And what about the inverted figure at bars 18 and 20? Do the three isolated semiquaver phrasings in the D minor Prelude (shown in Example 4c) mean that all the other semiquavers should be played in a detached manner? Why are all the quavers in the first bar of the F major Prelude slurred, and in groups of four? (see Example 4d.) Does this indicate that a player would normally have separated them, and that Bach wished the entire piece to be played legato? Or was the first quaver in each group of four to be held somewhat longer than the other three, to accent (by duration) the three beats in each bar?

### Rhythm and rubato: 'good' and 'bad' notes

We are so accustomed to thinking of rhythmic give and take as a characteristic of romantic music that the idea of a kind of rubato in baroque music may come as something of a surprise. Many seventeenth- and eighteenth-century books on composition and performance deal with the subject, however. They begin by making a distinction between *metre* (the exact, mathematical measurement of time) and *rhythm* (a flexible 'give and take' of notes within a

**Ex. 4**    Phrasings in J. S. Bach's *Das wohltemperirte Clavier*

regular metrical framework). The French used the word *mesure* to describe metre and *cadence* to describe rhythm.

Underlying the distinction between the two is the concept of 'good' and 'bad' notes, one that was already well developed by the end of the sixteenth century, when Girolamo Diruta published his *Il Transilvano*. It was restated in many seventeenth- and eighteenth-century treatises, including the *Praecepta*, a little book on theory and composition by Bach's cousin, J. G. Walther. It was still very much alive in such later books as Joachim Quantz's *Versuch einer Anweisung die Flöte traversière zu spielen* (Berlin, 1752),[7] where it is particularly clearly described, notably in the chapter 'On Good Execution in General in Singing and Playing'. Quantz begins by likening good musical performance to good oratory in which 'distinct and true pronunciation' are called for, together with appropriate vocal inflexions 'to arouse or still the passions' (chap. 11, paras. 1–3). He then applies these remarks to musical performance, particularly stressing the need for flexibility of rhythm.

> Here [he writes] some comment must be made on the length of time that is given to each note. You must know how to make a distinction in performance between the main notes – commonly called the accented notes ['frappantes'] or as the Italians say, *good* notes, and those that *pass*, which some foreigners call *bad* notes. Where possible, the main notes should always be emphasised more than the passing notes. For instance, if the semiquaver figures [Examples 5a and b] are played evenly, they will not sound as pleasing as if the first and third of each group were held somewhat longer than the second and fourth.

(a)

(b)

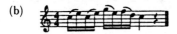

**Ex. 5**   Quantz: phrasing and rhythm

Quantz listed two exceptions to this: quick passages in a very fast movement, in which length and accent can be applied only to the first of every four notes; and all rapid vocal passagework, unless it is slurred. He stressed that on no account should 'good' notes be lengthened to the point that they sound like dotted notes. He was of course twelve years younger than Bach, and his musical style was considerably more 'modern' than Bach's. Even so, his comments here are very much in line with a tradition that can be traced back through the seventeenth century to Frescobaldi and beyond. Its effect would have been a kind of rhythmic give-and-take, even more subtle and instinctive, perhaps, than Chopin's much praised rhythmic flexibility. Undoubtedly the most important lesson here for the modern performer is that the shaping of line was a matter of rhythmic control rather than dynamic accent.[8]

### Legato and staccato

Perhaps the single most difficult problem to resolve is the extent to which non-legato articulation would have been used in performance. There was certainly general agreement that articulation should reflect the character of the piece being played. Johann Mattheson, a contemporary of J. S. Bach's, for instance, advised that the liveliness of allegros should normally be expressed by detached notes, and the tenderness of adagios by sustained, slurred notes. He also observed that a highly articulated ['viel punctirtes'] style, especially in lyrical pieces, has little or no *flowing* quality, and is to be avoided . . . Entrées and dances of a similarly elevated character, and even some overtures, on the other hand, positively demand detached articulation that is fresh, vivacious and well suited to joyful and energetic music.[9]

Mattheson considered Bach to be the greatest keyboard player of the time. Mattheson's comments, therefore, would seem to be particularly relevant. But what, we may well ask, is to be understood by 'detached' articulation? In what ways might it have differed from legato and staccato?

Quantz and C. P. E. Bach seem to have had three levels of articulation in mind. The outer extremes were staccato and legato.

When notes are to be detached [C. P. E. Bach explains], strokes or dots are placed above them [Example 6a] . . . and the notes are held for a little less than half their notated value. Legato notes are held for their full length, a slur being placed above them [Examples 6b and c] (chap. 3, paras. 17–18).

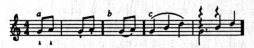

**Ex. 6**   C. P. E. Bach: slurs and articulation marks

This much is clear enough. But what about all the notes that are not marked in any way – the notes, that is, which belong to the middle category of Bach's three levels of articulation? It is here that Bach's advice comes as something of a shock.

Notes that are neither detached, connected nor fully held are sounded for *half* their value unless the abbreviation *ten[uto]* is written over them, in which case they must be held fully. Crotchets and quavers in moderate and slow speeds are usually performed in this semi-detached manner.

Quantz has similar advice to offer, notably in chapters 9 (paras. 10–11) and 17 (paras. 4, 8 and 26). Of course, both composers are writing about music that in style is far less contrapuntal than Bach's. Even so, their remarks certainly do not seem out of line with the fingering and phrasing evidence that has been discussed above. A sustained, singing legato would have been an essential ingredient of an expressive adagio, to be sure, but it would have been considered quite inappropriate for most other kinds of music.

How then does all this relate to, say, the interpretation of the '48'? Let us turn for a moment to some fingerings supplied by Harold Samuels in his 1924 Associated Board edition of the C major Prelude and Fugue of Book 2 (Example 7).

To begin with, there will be no need for that rather agonising attempt at the perfect legato, represented, for instance, by the left-hand finger shuffling

**Ex. 7**   J. S. Bach, Praeludium BWV 870, fingered by Samuels (bars 11–14)

in bar 12. If the fingers are suitably relaxed, the fifth finger can easily be transferred from the previous G to A. There will certainly be a tiny gap between the two notes (it need be no more than tiny) but it is one that Vogler's fingerings in other similar contexts inevitably produce. Nor will the rather extended hand stretch be needed in the left-hand line of bar 13; Vogler would certainly have lifted the little finger from the upbeat A of bar 12 to the downbeat D following; he might even have placed thumbs on the successive A–B flat–A quavers above the D. Just how big the resultant gaps between notes ought to be will depend of course on the player's concept of the piece: whether the fugue belongs more to the category of the lively allegro or the tender adagio, for Bach has left no guidelines in the score as to speed or mood. Gaps there will certainly be, however; and if Mattheson, C. P. E. Bach and Quantz are to be believed, the gaps could under certain circumstances be half the written values of the notes.

### ANALYSIS AS AN INTERPRETATIVE TOOL

It may seem odd that Bach was content to leave the player to decide the speed and character of each prelude and fugue – odd, because many composers (especially the French) were by then using a wide vocabulary of Italian and French terms to suggest musical moods. There are no tempo or 'mood' markings of any kind though in the '48', apart from the B minor Fugue of Book 1 and the G minor Prelude of Book 2, both of which are marked 'Largo'. Yet a quick comparison of current recordings suggests that players rarely disagree fundamentally on questions of speed and mood. Few players, for instance, would quarrel with Tovey for suggesting 'andante con moto ma largamente' as an appropriate marking for the C major Prelude of Book 2.

What then is it that makes for this common ground of understanding? Why did Tovey feel a slowish pace to be appropriate here, and why did he choose to qualify it with 'ma largamente'? Questions such as these lead inevitably from the study of external performance evidence to an examination of the internal evidence of the notes themselves, and to what is generally known as musical analysis.

Analysis is so often thought of as a dry and irrelevant academic pursuit in which music is simply pigeonholed into one of a number of recognised forms: da capo arias, rondos, first movement sonata forms and so on. Properly handled, however, analysis ought almost to be an act of creation, in which the analyst becomes as it were the composer, following each stage of the process of composition through from beginning to end. The business of composition, after all, is the communication of musical ideas to the listener – motives or figures, themes, rhythms, harmonies and textures. There has to be a logical shape to the music, otherwise the composition would not hang together. Most compositions create expectations which are in various ways fulfilled (ultimately, if not immediately). Most music is dramatic in the sense that there are tensions and resolutions, climaxes and relaxations. The performer has to understand how all these are achieved, if the performance is to be fully convincing.

It is all too easy in analysing a piece to become preoccupied with details and to miss the shape of the composition as a whole: we fail to see the shape of the wood, in other words, because we are so busy looking at each individual tree. As far as performance is concerned, the shape of the wood is vitally important. Take the C major Prelude, for example. It *looks* complicated. For much of the time there are four separate strands of melody, all made up of lots of short motives. The basically triadic harmony is embellished with passing notes and suspensions. None of these details should be ignored, to be sure. The first thing to do, however, is to try to see the broad shape of the piece. 'Shape', in the present sense, has little to do with whether the piece is in binary, ternary, rondo or first movement form. It is rather the music's *dramatic* shape: its moments of tension and relaxation, its climaxes, its changes of pace and mood.

One element that plays a particularly important role in the shaping of this Prelude is tessitura – the rise and fall, that is, of its melodic lines. In a sense, musical notation is a kind of graph of pitch: if the C major Prelude were compressed on to one line, it might look something like Example 8.

For the first seven bars the general direction of the upper line is downward. The direction then reverses, rising first to bar 10, and then to a much higher peak at 15. A further downward movement then occurs from 15 to 21, followed by a rise to an all-time peak between bars 25 and 28. A final gentle decline brings the music back to mid-range – its starting point.

Tessitura alone would be insufficient to account for the feeling of tension

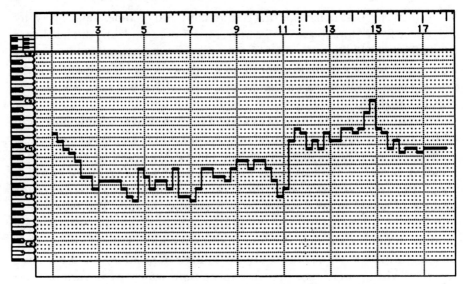

**Ex. 8**   The upper line of Bach's Praeludium BWV 870 in graph form (bars 1–18)

and release that is in the music, however: other factors also contribute to that feeling. The more important of these are the tonal scheme, the harmonic rhythm (i.e. the frequency at which the harmonies change), the rhythmic and melodic character of the motives or figures and the interplay between concord and dissonance.

### The tonal scheme

Like almost all eighteenth- and nineteenth-century compositions, the C major Prelude sets out from a clearly defined key (in this case, C major), it goes through related keys, and it finally returns to the key in which it started. The gentle forward movement of the music never stops until the final cadence. Nevertheless, at certain points there is a sense of arrival at a new key. There is a sense, too, at these points that the original tonic of C is being ousted by related keys, notably where there are perfect cadences: there are two such important cadences, in bars 11–13, where the music very clearly has modulated into D minor, and 25–7, where the key of G minor is established. Moreover, both cadences are reinforced by colourful flattened supertonic progressions which occur just beforehand (see bars 11:3–4, and 26:1–2). It is close to these perfect cadences that the peaks of the melodic climaxes occur. Simple as the tonal scheme of the Prelude is, it does, nonetheless, illustrate one very important and characteristic feature of Bach's music, namely the move further and further away from the tonic key as the music progresses. During the first melodic climax the music goes into

D minor, one flat away from the original key; during the second climax it goes to G minor, two flats away. In some of Bach's more intense fugues, the music goes through even more remote keys shortly before the final return to the tonic, and at the same time the pace of the modulation accelerates, as for instance in the A flat Fugue of Book 2 of the '48' and the great C major organ Fugue BWV 547. The shift further and further away from the tonic can heighten the tension of the music considerably. As a tonal dramatist, Bach had no equal.

   Once or twice in the C major Prelude the harmonies arouse expectations of arrival at a new key, but they then fail to settle in the expected key. This is particularly obvious in bar 10, where the effect is to stretch the musical phrase beyond its expected span, thus adding to the mounting tension of the next three bars. An awareness of cadence and of those moments when the expected cadence fails to materialise are essential if the music is to be phrased and paced properly. The arrival chords, incidentally, will almost always be felt as 'good' notes: that is, they will normally fall on an accented beat and be heard as important notes of the phrases to which they belong. The player may well feel that some slight stressing of these 'good' chords is appropriate in the manner described above. In using a slight give and take, according to the principles of 'good' and 'bad' notes, however, care should be taken not to interrupt the sense of forward movement.

*Harmonic rhythm*

The independence of the four voices, which are dissonant in many places, may obscure the fact that the music is built upon a slowly moving series of chords (most of these are simple triads, but there are some dominant sevenths, diminished sevenths and augmented triads as well). Consider the harmonies of the opening bars (Example 9). There are rarely more than four chord changes to the bar, whilst in many bars there are just two or three. It is this steady spaciousness of harmonic movement that Tovey must have had in mind when he placed 'Andante con moto, ma largamente' at the head of the Prelude, as a suggestion of how the music ought to be played. During the course of the piece the pace of harmonic change remains fairly steady. Nonetheless, there is some increase in activity between bars 10 and 18 and between bars 25 and 29, the locations of the two climaxes.

**Ex. 9**   The harmonic flow of the opening bars of the Praeludium BWV 870

### The motives or figures

The most important of the handful of melodic motives upon which this piece is built is the group of three rising semiquavers in the first bar. This figure repeatedly occurs in various guises throughout the Prelude. Two other motives are also of some importance: a little arpeggio figure of semiquavers (see for instance 2iiRH, 5ivLH, 8iiLH, 10iiLH, 11ivRH and 16ivRH)[10] and a small, inward-turning group of semiquavers (as in 2ivRH, 3ivLH and 8iLH). The way in which the piece is built out of small rhythmic and melodic motives is entirely typical of the time, and it is not unconnected with a baroque theory of expression which came to be known as the *Affektenlehre*, or 'Doctrine of the affections'. It had its origins in the ancient art of public speaking, the idea being that the orator would draw from a large repertory of phrases or figures of speech the ones that would most impress and move the hearer. Descriptions of musical 'figures' (*figurae*) are to be found in many seventeenth- and early eighteenth-century books on music.[11] These figures were small groups of notes having very clearly defined shapes; the *figura suspirans*, for instance, consists of an upbeat group of short notes leading to a downbeat stress – the upbeat group typically starts after a brief rest (e.g.

). Many such figures are to be found in the C major Prelude.

### Consonance and dissonance

In the case of the C major Prelude, the flavour of the main figure comes not only from its melodic shape, but, as we shall see, from the way in which that shape is fitted into the harmony. Dissonance can be very expressive (i.e. *affective*). The C major Prelude is full of passing and suspended dissonance. Some of the passing dissonance falls on the weakest parts of the bar; in the left-hand stave of bar 13, for instance, the semiquaver G passes between the chord notes F and A; it occurs on the weak second semiquaver of the crotchet beat (rather than on the stronger first or third semiquaver). Many of the passing dissonances in this piece do, however, fall on the first and third notes (i.e. the relatively 'good' notes), especially those developed from the principal figure which opens the piece. The offbeat beginning of this figure is evident enough; what is less evident, yet perhaps of greater importance, is the manner in which the second of the three semiquavers is almost always dissonant: this note falls on the third semiquaver of the crotchet and is relatively more accented than those before and after it. The dissonance has the quality of a small accent that gently propels the music forward, as in bars 4i, 5iii, 7ii, 8i and 9iii.

The Prelude is also full of suspended dissonances, which again have the effect of pushing the music forward. The first of these occurs in the fourth bar, the E hanging over from the previous C major chord and then resolving on the first inversion of D minor. Three suspensions follow in close succession, establishing the home key of C major (bars 4i/5i/5ii). From this point onwards to the very end, the texture is full of suspensions, adding richness to the sonority and projecting the music continuously forward. Indeed, these suspensions are so prominent that they almost assume the role of independent 'figures'. They certainly contribute a great deal to the overall 'affect' of the Prelude.

## The form of the Prelude

This brief analysis began by playing down the importance of 'form spotting', for analysis is much more than the identification of conventional forms. The very search for set forms can indeed lead to the misleading idea that there were pre-existent moulds into which composers simply poured their music. Nonetheless, this aspect of composition cannot be ignored entirely. In the case of the C major Prelude Bach has used none of the normal baroque forms. Its most important feature is the restatement of bars 6–13 in bars 20iii–28iii. The music is not simply repeated, however, but is transposed up a fourth. The repeat, therefore, sounds brighter; at bar 22, moreover, Bach gives extra rhythmic impetus to the textures (cf. bar 8), thus heightening the impact.

Czerny evidently had his own ideas about the flow of the music when he added expression marks to his edition (see p. 11). There can be no *one* way of doing this, of course, but there are places in the Prelude where he has perhaps misunderstood the logic of the construction. A *piano* opening is quite possible, surely. But should the crescendo begin perhaps in bar 7? Should the *forte* at 9 be reserved for the second half of bar 12? Should there be a small diminuendo in bars 15–16? Despite the increased chromaticism in bars 18–20, is Czerny's crescendo justified? To answer questions of this kind satisfactorily demands instinctive musicianship and analytical insights of a high order.

# 3

## Corelli's Violin Sonata Op. 5 No. 11

NATIONAL STYLES OF STRING PLAYING

Two national schools of composition dominated early eighteenth-century Europe: the French and the Italian. Each boasted its own style of music, its own style of performance and even, in certain cases, its own types of musical instrument. No composer could wholly avoid the influence of the two great schools. Indeed, much that the greatest composers wrote cannot properly be understood without some appreciation of the distinctive qualities of French and Italian music. The cosmopolitan composer and keyboard virtuoso Johann Jacob Froberger wrote to Paris in 1650 for dance suites by the French composer Chambonnières, which he studied before he composed his own. Two highly influential German composers, Georg Muffat (1653–1704) and J. S. Kusser (1660–1727), spent several years in Paris studying with Lully. Muffat later visited Italy to study the art of writing Italian-style concertos with Corelli and Pasquini. Bach copied out all six of Dieupart's harpsichord suites before beginning work on his first important set of keyboard dances, the so-called 'English' suites. Not long after that he set about the task of transcribing for solo keyboard orchestral concertos by such composers as Vivaldi and Telemann; his own music at about this time begins unmistakably to show Italian influences. Clearly, then, the issue of national styles must figure prominently in the following pages.

### The modern and eighteenth-century violin families compared

As we shall see below, eighteenth-century listeners found considerable differences between the sounds of Italian and French string groups. Before discussing this, however, a preliminary word is needed about the even greater differences between 'period' and modern strings. In part the differences are structural in origin. The eighteenth-century violin was strung with gut, not wire. Performance pitch was variable, but it tended to be somewhat lower than the modern A=440 (see below, p. 154). There was consequently less tension on the bridge and soundboard, which meant that the bass bar supporting the soundboard could be of lighter construction, as could the soundpost that transmitted the string vibrations from soundboard to belly. Differences in bow design were of even greater importance. There was less hair, the hair width was narrower, the tension was far less than that of a modern Tourte bow, and the point of balance was different. The sum of all this was a lighter, less ringing and less legato sound.[1]

The most important witness to the differences between French and Italian styles of string playing is the German Kapellmeister and composer Georg Muffat. During the 1680s and 1690s he published several sets of compositions: two, the *Armonico tributo* (Salzburg, 1682) and the *Auserlesene Instrumental-Music* (Passau, 1701, reproduced in *Denkmäler der Tonkunst in Oesterreich* XI), contain music in the Italian style; another two, the *Florilegium Primum* (Augsburg, 1695, *D.T.Ö.*I) and *Florilegium Secundum* (Passau, 1698, *D.T.Ö.* II), contain ensemble suites in the French style. So concerned was he about the failure of his contemporaries to distinguish between the French and Italian styles that he published detailed performance instructions in the 1689 and 1701 collections.[2]

On two points the French and the Italians were agreed: first, that disciplined, unanimous bowing was of fundamental importance to good ensemble performance; and second, that bow strokes should be as 'long, steady, sweet and even' as possible. In the *Auserlesene Instrumental-Music* Muffat described having heard Corelli's concertos played in Rome with the utmost accuracy by a large group of players. Corelli's pupil Geminiani later wrote of his master's insistence upon uniformity of bowing in ensemble music. Muffat similarly tells of the tightly disciplined bowing of Lully's famous Parisian ensemble, *Les petits-violons du Roi*.

However, whilst both the Italians and the French were aiming for technical perfection, there clearly was a world of difference between the sounds of French and Italian string groups. Muffat made the particular point in the preface to his *Florilegium Secundum* that the Italians exploited extremes of tempo, dynamics and articulation in their concern to create an appropriate sense of drama:

> The Italians [he wrote] . . . are accustomed to proceed much more slowly than we do in the directions *Adagio, Grave, Largo*, etc., – so slowly sometimes that one can scarcely wait for them; but at the directions *Vivace, Presto, Piu Presto* and *Prestissimo* much more rapidly and in a lively manner. For by exactly observing this opposition or rivalry of the slow and the fast, the loud and the soft, the fullness of the great choir and the delicacy of the little trio, the ear is ravished by a singular astonishment, as is the eye by the opposition of light and shade. [Muffat is here referring to the concerto, of course.] Though this has often been reported by others, it can never be said or enjoined sufficiently.

The French critic Raguenet particularly emphasised the sheer volume that Italian players managed to get out of their instruments:

> The Italians have ... the same advantage over us in respect of the instruments and performers as they have in respect of the singers and their voices. Their violins are mounted with strings much larger than ours; their bows are longer and they can make their instruments sound as loud again as we do ours. The first time I heard our band in the Opera after my return out of Italy, my ears had been so used to the loudness of the Italian violins that I thought ours had all been bridled [muted] ... Their bass-viols are as large again as the French, and all ours put together don't sound so loud as two or three of those basses do in Italy.[3]

### Bowing

The smaller sound of French strings resulted, at least in part, from bowing techniques, as Muffat explained in the preface to his *Florilegium Secundum*:

> Most German violinists ... hold the bow as the French do, pressing the hair with the thumb and resting the other fingers on the stick of the bow: the French do the same when playing the bass. Italian violinists [the term refers to players of all bowed instruments smaller than the gamba and cello], on the other hand, never touch the bow hair, whilst Italian gamba players and bass players place their fingers between the hair and the wood.

In other words, the French bow hold tended to produce a shorter bow stroke and thus a more detached quality of articulation.

Equally important to articulation was the matter of bow direction. If Muffat is to be believed, the French differed from the Italians in consistently placing the downbow on the first note of each bar. This convention may well have arisen from the fact that the French had first used the violin to accompany dancing. A strongly articulated, first-beat downbow would certainly have provided the sort of rhythmic pulse that a dancer would have appreciated. According to Muffat, the Lullists regarded the downbow rule as central to the entire art of bowing. The Italians, on the other hand, applied it far less rigorously. To illustrate his point, Muffat bowed a short melody, first as an Italian might have done it and then in the French manner, a downbow being placed on the first beat of every bar (see Example 10).

**Ex. 10**  Muffat's Italian and French bowings

The French bowings tend to produce a more detached line: see, for instance, the two downbows crossing bars 3–4 and 5–6 and the successive upbows in bars 2, 4 and 6. Both the French and Italian bowings do, however, articulate the line; there is no suggestion here of an endless bow.

In the preface to his *Florilegium Secundum* Muffat shows exactly how a French string player would have tackled various rhythmic patterns to ensure a regular downbow on the first beat. His examples (11a–n below) speak for themselves: they illustrate, in turn, separate, alternate strokes (a–b); contexts in which two downbows follow each other (c–e); the *craquer* technique in which two upbows follow in succession (f–i); and some exceptional circumstances in which the downbow rule might be ignored (j–k). Examples (l–n) are of especial interest, for they show ways in which three popular dances could be bowed.

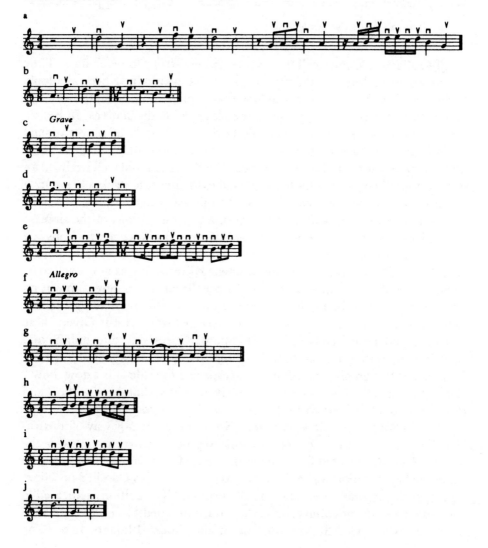

**Ex. 11**   Muffat's bowing principles

All Muffat's examples call for a separate bow stroke for each note. They do, nonetheless, illustrate the type of choice that would have been available to the player within the downbeat/downbow convention. Even the strictest application of the principle presents the player with alternatives. In Example 11c, for instance, the bowing could be down/up/up if the player wished to place less emphasis on the upbeat. An Italian mode of bowing considerably increases the available alternatives. The Bourrée could well begin on an upbow, the subsequent notes being played with alternate strokes to secure a downbow on the syncopated minim C. In this way interpretative decisions can be made, working within the performance conventions of the time.

The lack of slurred examples in the Muffat performance instructions is a reminder that slurring was then very much regarded as an ornament, and that slurs had little (if any) function as bowing directions – as devices, that is, to place downbows on downbeats. And since the slurred note-group was an ornament, it had to be made to sound as one, notably by holding the first note slightly longer than its true value (see below, p. 126). Given these generally understood conventions, it is hardly surprising that upbow and downbow markings are rarely to be found in contemporary sources. Both French and Italian players would have respected the rule of the downbow – the French, strictly, the Italians more freely, provided that the downbow and downbeat coincided comfortably every two bars or so.

Corelli's Sonata for solo violin Op. 5 No. 11 may serve by way of illustration. The first concern, of course, must be to procure an accurate text of the sonata. A clearly printed facsimile of the first edition would in this case be quite the best solution, since there are no problems with Corelli's notation, and since the originals are so beautifully printed.[4] The edition, dedicated to the Electress of Brandenburg, Sofia Carlotta, and dated 1700, was published in Rome, where Corelli was working at the time. Although there is no evidence that Corelli checked the printed text before publication, there is no reason to suppose that he would have been any less exacting here than he was in ensuring that unanimity of bowing for which his players were so famous. One should avoid at all costs the kind of romantic edition represented in Example 12 (E. G. Pigott, 1849).

**Ex. 12**   Corelli, Sonata Op. 5 No. 11: a nineteenth-century edition compared with the original

The opening Preludio of the sonata may be bowed as it comes. Provided that upbeats following rests are played with upbows (as in bars 3 and 4), a downbow occurs on the first note of every bar, up to bar 15. At this point one bowing decision is conceivable, though by no means essential: a *craquer* upbow on the first quaver E of that bar, to ensure that the last bar comes out on the downbow. In the following Allegro (Example 13) only three bowing-direction decisions are inescapable: to retake downbows at the beginning of bars 15, 17 and 25. Note the way in which bars 1–4 come out right, no bowing retakes being necessary.

Ex. 13    Corelli, Op. 5 No. 11: Allegro

The third movement, a 3/2 Adagio, is a typically Italianate skeleton upon which the player would have improvised: more will be said about this below (see p. 41). The succeeding Vivace is in 3/8 time (Example 14). Its opening phrase well illustrates the alternatives that are available within the Italian bowing method. It is certainly playable as it comes (solution 1), downbows fitting the shape of the line well (see especially the syncopation in bars 1 and

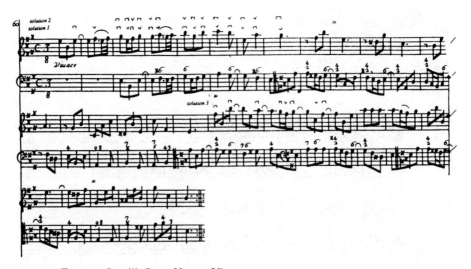

Ex. 14    Corelli, Op. 5 No. 11: Vivace

2, and the repeated G sharp at the beginning of bar 4). The phrase could be bowed as in solution 2, retaking a downbow on the second note of bar 3; this solution would perhaps suggest itself if the phrase were to be interpreted in an increasingly articulated manner, greater weight being given to the second slurred group than to the first. The bowing will also depend to some extent on how the accentuation of bars 6 to 7 is seen: is more weight to be placed on the C sharp and E than on the A? If so, solution 2 might again be adopted. Are, for instance, the syncopations to be emphasised? If so, the bowing might well work out as 3 (bars 20–3). The bowed semiquavers in bar 26 suggest that Corelli would have played the entire passage from bar 25 as it comes right up to the double bar (starting on a downbow). Nonetheless, other solutions are certainly possible. The one definitely wrong decision would be to add slurs to a text that gives every impression of having been carefully prepared. In the last movement, a Gavotta, there is no slurring except in the final four bars. There, most unusually, a slur is to be found covering a total of 24 semiquavers and crossing bars 12–15. As we shall later see, baroque string slurring rarely crosses the barline: a slur that crosses no fewer than three barlines is quite exceptional.

One or two passages from other sonatas in the Op. 5 set may serve to cover those general principles of bowing that are not encountered in the Eleventh Sonata. Compound metres present the player with the greatest number of bowing alternatives. The quavers in the Giga of the Fifth Sonata (Example 15), for instance, are almost wholly bowed in groups of three, whilst in the Giga of the Seventh Sonata (Example 16) they are bowed in groups of two plus one.

**Ex. 15**   Corelli, Op. 5 No. 5: Giga

**Ex. 16**   Corelli, Op. 5 No. 7: Giga

**Ex. 17**    Corelli, Op. 5 No. 3: Allegro (finale)

The bowings of both movements are unambiguous and easy to follow. The 12/8 finale of the Third Sonata (Example 17), on the other hand, is less straightforward. It is built on two fairly similar figures. The first involves a changing-note pattern of three bowed quavers. The second takes the form of unbowed, broken chord figuration. After the sixth bar, the second figure predominates. The first does appear here and there, however: just before the double bar, for instance (bars 15–16), at the A minor cadence in bar 22 and especially in the closing four bars. Yet no slurs are printed beyond the sixth bar. Are the bowings in the first six bars then to be regarded as the pattern to be continued after bar 6? This, after all, was Bach's occasional practice and it was one that C. P. E. Bach later endorsed (see p. 14). No firm answer is possible, but it is worth seeing what Corelli did in other similar movements. In the finales of the Fifth and Sixth Sonatas, for instance, obvious as the figuration is, it is fully slurred. Perhaps, therefore, no slurs should be added to the finale of the Third Sonata? This then leaves the problem of how to play the unslurred quavers. Much will depend on the speed at which the movement is taken. In the present case, since the speed is going to be fairly fast (four in a bar rather than twelve), the most comfortable bowing is going to be as it comes. Two other bowings are, nonetheless, theoretically possible: down/up/up, down/up/up, using the *craquer* upbow technique; and down/up/down/, down/up/down. These bowings are better suited to slower speeds, however, the choice depending on the weight that is to be given to the second and third quavers of each group.

In conclusion, the thirteenth variation of the Twelfth Sonata ('La Follia') is an apt reminder that the player should intervene no more than is absolutely necessary to ensure a workable bowing, for, complex as it is, this passage can be played exactly as it comes (Example 18).

**Ex. 18**   Corelli, Op. 5 No. 12

Two important aspects of violin technique go unmentioned up to the time of Geminiani and Leopold Mozart: fingering and intonation. If Leopold Mozart is a reliable authority for earlier fingering practice (and he may well not be), care was taken when playing prominent melodic lines to achieve as even a tone as possible. This involved remaining on one string where practicable, and rigorously avoiding open strings, which were observed to produce quite a different timbre to that of stopped strings. As to intonation, both Geminiani and Mozart discussed the difference between the major and minor semitone, as did so many of their contemporaries (see below for Quantz, p. 154, and Tosi, p. 83). As Mozart put it:

> On the keyboard, G sharp and A flat, C sharp and D flat, F sharp and G flat, and so on, are one and the same note. This is caused by the temperament. But according to the right ratio, all the notes lowered by a flat are a comma higher than those that are raised by a sharp. For example, D flat is higher than C sharp... Here a good ear must be the judge, and it would indeed be well to introduce pupils to the monochord. (*Versuch*, chap. 3, para. 6)

### *AFFEKT*: TEMPO AND DYNAMICS

One expressive principle is common to much baroque music, be it instrumental or vocal: that there is normally a consistency of mood within a single movement, even though fluctuating tensions and relaxations may temper that mood. There is little or none of the emotional confrontation *within* a movement that characterises so much music of the Romantic era. Failure to accept this fact led 'romantic' editors like Pigott (Example 13 above) to superimpose on baroque music dynamic contrasts, speed variations and phrasings that simply bear no relation to what the composer was actually doing.

The Italian ritornello aria is perhaps the most striking example of motivic (and thus 'affective') unity. In both opera and oratorio of the high baroque the aria became the principal vehicle for the demonstration of *Affekt*, or mood. It was in the aria that characterisation and motivation were revealed. It was in the aria that emotional reactions to the events of the moment were displayed. An 'affekt'ive composition was one in which the motives – the *figurae* – were memorable and appropriate in spirit to the dramatic situation.[5]

A well-known ritornello aria from Handel's *Messiah* may serve as an example. 'O thou that tellest good tidings to Zion' opens with twelve instrumental bars in which two figures (A and B) are introduced: A forms the basis of the vocal line; B is violinistic in character, and it is reserved for the upper strings. The leaping quality of B and its continuous semiquaver motion are obviously appropriate to the joyful text: the surging line even seems to paint the words of the second phrase, 'get thee up into the high mountain' (Example 19). After an extended instrumental introduction, or 'ritornello' (so named because it returns in various guises through the movement), the solo voice enters, the scene having been set, so to speak. There follows a continuous dialogue between voice and instruments. Towards the middle of the piece the music modulates to A major (the dominant key); there is a second instrumental ritornello in which only B is developed. Further dialogue between voice and instruments leads to a brief ritornello in the subdominant (G), and thence back to the tonic of D major. At this point there would normally be a repeat of the opening ritornello; Handel, however, replaces this by a substantial chorus, again based on A.

The da capo aria was a particularly popular type of ritornello aria, having the shape ABA – A ending in the tonic with the opening instrumental ritornello, B being in a contrasting, related key. This type of aria did in fact offer useful opportunities for mood contrast: 'He was despised' is a well-known case. The point is, however, that within each section the *Affekt* remains constant. Movements in which there is actually an element of dialogue between contrasting *Affekte* (such as the very first Allegro from Handel's Concerto Grosso Op. 6 No. 1) are rare.

The ritornello principle came to dominate large-scale compositions of the high baroque – both vocal and instrumental. It underlies, for instance, all the concerto forms of Vivaldi, Bach and Handel; it is the basis for many of Bach's most extended fugues, and it is even to be found in some of Bach's larger organ preludes.

The second important form of the high baroque is the binary movement. Practically all dances come to rest at a double bar near the middle of the piece, either on the tonic or the dominant, or in a closely related key. The first half is then repeated, as also is the second. Neither repeat is written out but is simply indicated by repeat marks. Like ritornello and da capo structures, binary pieces are normally built up from two or three short figures, in which there is a homogeneity of mood.

The third 'form' – fugue – is more in the nature of a principle than a structure. It too is built out of a handful of figures that make up the subject and perhaps one or more countersubjects. Its dynamic shape may be climactic – as is the case with Bach's magnificent B minor triple fugue for organ, which comes to an impressive climax in the third section. But again there is

**Ex. 19**  Handel, *Messiah*: 'O thou that tellest'

no dramatic contrast of the kind to be found, for instance, in the first movement of Beethoven's 'Pathétique' Sonata.

What, then, does this have to tell the performer? There are, perhaps, two major points. If it is true that baroque structures are based, not on large-scale oppositions of contrasting materials but on short one- and two-bar figures, then it is wrong to superimpose romantically inspired schemes of dynamic contrast on such music. Secondly, if baroque compositions are built

from small-scale figures, then baroque performance must start by consider-
ing how these are to be articulated. To be sure, the performer must constantly be aware of the ways in which large-scale phrase structure is defined by
cadence. A performance can only be effective, however, if the figures are
imaginatively handled.

The way in which structural principles developed as time went on is
obvious enough from even the most cursory comparisons of late seventeenth-
and early eighteenth-century compositions. The figures of Corelli's Op. 5
Sonatas are far less sharply defined than are those of Handel's Op. 1
Sonatas. There is less motivic unity and more random figuration. Key
ranges are more restricted, and cadences are less varied. Yet in Corelli's
Sonata Op. 5 No. 11, discussed above, the basic features are all evident. The
short Preludio is the least coherent of the movements. Its semi-
improvisatory upper line falls into three very loosely defined sections; these
are established by the V–I cadences in bars 6 (B major), 9–10 (C sharp
minor) and 16. In terms of figures, the first six bars do have a loose sense of
unity, as do bars 6–10, and 10–16. Perhaps the most cohesive element of the
Adagio is the running bass. The second movement is dominated by a
striding arpeggio figure which appears in some form or other almost continuously, save for a brief episode in bars 25–30. The 3/8 Vivace is fugal, its
figure – the fugue subject – pervading the entire movement. In the closing
Gavotta there are two closely allied figures, one for each half of the very brief
movement.

### Tempo

Before the development of the metronome in 1815, attempts had been made
from time to time to devise a convenient way of measuring time accurately,
but with no great success. From 1700 onwards, words (mainly Italian and
French) were used with increasing frequency to give a general idea of what
was intended, but as Charles Avison observed:

> The words Andante, Presto, Allegro, etc., are differently applied in . . . differ-
> ent kinds of music. For the same terms which denote lively and gay in the opera
> or concert style, may be understood in the practice of church-music, as
> cheerful and serene, or if the reader pleases, less lively and gay; wherefore the
> Allegro etc. in this kind of composition should always be performed somewhat
> slower than is usual in concertos or operas.[6]

The six most common speeds in the music of Corelli, Handel, Bach and
Vivaldi are (from slow to fast) adagio, largo, andante, allegro, vivace, and
presto. All four composers used other terms as well, especially Vivaldi, who
went to incredible lengths to describe exactly what kind of speed he wanted.
Here, for instance, are some of his versions of allegro: allegro assai, allegro

molto, allegro e spiritoso, allegro con moto, allegro non molto, allegro ma cantabile, allegro poco, allegro ma poco, allegro ma poco e cantabile, allegro poco poco, allegro non troppo, allegro ma d'un mezzo tempo, allegro molto più che si puo.[7]

To arrange so many ambiguous terms in any sort of order would clearly be impossible. The relationship between the six principal tempo markings, however, is fairly clear – at least in the music of Corelli, Vivaldi, Handel and Bach. Despite certain conflicts of opinion in contemporary dictionaries, there is in fact only one minor problem: the relationship of adagio to largo. According to J. G. Walther, adagio was 'langsam' (slow) and largo 'sehr langsam' (very slow). Sebastian Brossard reversed the order, however. Nonetheless, Corelli, Handel, Bach and Vivaldi all followed an identical code of practice. When they qualified the two slowest terms, they made the adagio even slower (molto adagio, adagio assai, and adagissimo) and the largo a little less slow (larghetto, largo ma non tanto). The implication, then, is that adagio was slowest of all and largo a little less slow. Any doubt there may be about the relationship between the two fastest terms is similarly settled by the fact that Presto when qualified becomes faster, and Vivace slower. None of the Op. 5 Solo Sonatas presents any problems, the markings (as in the Eleventh Sonata) being mainly confined to Adagio, Allegro and Vivace.

Even when the speed is described in a primary source there is no guarantee that it represents the composer's final thoughts (if, indeed, composers before Beethoven did ever have 'final' thoughts!). Many baroque composers used Italian terms that are now commonly thought of as speed markings to suggest mood rather than speed. Handel, for instance, headed the third movement of his Sonata Op. 6 No. 8 Andante allegro: the combination could be taken to indicate either a fast-moving andante or a slowish allegro, or, more probably, a springy, cheerful andante ('allegro' literally means cheerful). Similar cases abound in the music of all the later baroque composers.[8]

Surprisingly enough, baroque dance movements (courante, allemande, sarabande and gigue) were played at all sorts of different speeds. Allemandes in Corelli's Op. 2 Trio Sonatas are variously headed Presto, Allegro, Largo and Adagio. The sarabandes of the Sonata da Camera Opp. 2 and 4 (1685 and 1694) carry equally diverse markings. The diversity of dance-movement speeds in music of the high baroque is illustrated in Table 1.

Corelli marked his dance movements with unusual care. Others, like Bach and Handel, tended only to give a title to the movement, leaving the player to decide on its speed and character. Some scholars have attempted to fill these gaps by studying the descriptions of dances in contemporary books on dancing. Corelli's diverse markings should be enough to prove the limitations of such an exercise! Clearly taste is the only arbiter here, taste informed by an understanding of the rate at which the harmonies change, the charac-

ter of the figures, the type of texture, and by such external factors as the
acoustics of the building in which the performance is taking place, and even
*the nature of the occasion!*

Table 1.⁹ Some speed markings in late seventeenth- and
early eighteenth-century dance movements

|  | Adagio | Largo | Allegro | Vivace | Presto |
|---|---|---|---|---|---|
| Allemande | 16 | 6 | 37 | 1 | 7 |
| Courante | 6 | 3 | 47 | 8 | 6 |
| Sarabande | 14 | 33*a* | 12 | 2 | 14 |
| Gigue | 0 | 4 | 46 | 8 | 46 |

*a*includes Grave.
(These figures are drawn from a study of more than one hundred
diverse baroque publications.)

DYNAMICS

Throughout the fifty or so movements of Corelli's Op. 5 Solo Sonatas there
are less than thirty dynamic markings. This is altogether characteristic of the
composer. From the time of Corelli onwards a steady increase is observable
in the use of such markings, and in subtle shadings of dynamic, as Table 2
clearly suggests:

Table 2.¹⁰ The principal dynamic markings used by
Corelli, Handel, Vivaldi and Bach

|  | Corelli | Handel | Bach | Vivaldi |
|---|---|---|---|---|
| *f molto* | − | − | − | + |
| *f (forte)* | + | + | + | + |
| *ff* | − | − | − | + |
| *poco forte* | − | − | 1713?*a* | + |
| *mf* | ? | ? | + | + |
| *mp* | ? | ? | − | + |
| *poco piano* | − | − | + | − |
| *quasi piano* | − | − | − | + |
| *piano assai* | − | − | − | + |
| *p (piano)* | + | + | + | + |
| *pp (piu piano)* | − | + | + | + |
| *piano molto* | − | − | − | + |
| *piano piano* | − | − | + | − |
| *pianissimo (p)* | − | ? | + | + |

*a*Queries indicate uncertainty as to the authenticity of the
markings.

Nonetheless, the subtler shadings are far outweighed by two basic markings
– *piano* and *forte* – the only two that Corelli is known for certain to have used.
    It has been argued that baroque dynamics should be terraced, since there

are no baroque signs for getting louder and softer. Indeed, on two important instruments – the harpsichord and the organ – crescendos and diminuendos are impossible. They can be accomplished, however, on all other instruments, including the clavichord, which was capable of the most subtle gradations of tone, and which was a very popular instrument in the German-speaking states. There is, moreover, telling evidence that Italian orchestral dynamics were anything but terraced. Scipione Maffei, writing from Rome in 1711, had this to say, for example, about the way that the Italians played:

> It is known to everyone who delights in music that one of the principal means by which the skillful in that art derive the secret of especially delighting those who listen, is the *piano* and *forte* in the theme and its response, in the gradual diminution of tone little by little, and in the sudden return to the full power of the instrument; this is frequently practised with marvellous effect in the great concerts at Rome.[11]

At that time Corelli himself was one of the leading violin virtuosi in Rome, and he directed many of its most important concerts. Indeed, it is more than likely that Maffei had him in mind, even though he did not specifically name him. Clearly, then, the Italians put very much more into a performance than appeared on the printed page!

Most of Corelli's movements lack an initial dynamic marking, as do so many others of the period. Invariably the first mark to appear during the course of a movement is a *piano*, from which it may be concluded that *forte* was the normal level at which a piece was started. In the Op. 5 No. 11 Sonata, for instance, the very first marking (*piano*) occurs at bar 17 of the second movement, and it takes the form of an echo repeat of the previous two bars. There is another such echo repeat in bars 28–30, after the double bar. Corelli was rather fond of ending a sonata quietly (if only perhaps for the reason that a loud ending would have been more expected!): *piano* markings covering the last four bars or so are to be found in six of the twelve sonatas. When something other than an opening *forte* was required, it was commonly indicated in the title or the tempo marking of the movement: thus, for instance, a section of the third movement of Handel's Concerto Grosso Op. 6 No. 2 is headed 'Larghetto andante, e piano', but no dynamic marking is placed beneath the actual notes.

Johann Walther defined *forte* as a 'strong' but 'natural' dynamic, in which the voices or instruments were not 'forced', a definition that was echoed in other contemporary works of reference.[12] Vivaldi's *f molto* was in fact a special effect, having a descriptive function, as for instance in the Op. 8 No. 5 Concerto, 'La tempesta di mare'. We may well question, then, the search by many twentieth-century virtuosi for the 'big sound'. Baroque musicians liked a full yet intimately warm sound, not an intense and intrusive one.

During the late seventeenth and early eighteenth centuries, *forte* seems to have been used to indicate a normal and very general dynamic level rather than a precise degree of loudness. It was contrasted with *piano*, which Walther defined as an 'echo'. *Piú piano*, according to him, was a 'second echo' sounding much further away than *piano*, and *pianissimo* a third echo, in which the sound of the voice or instrument fades into the air. The normal *forte*, then, probably covered quite a broad dynamic range within which a great deal of nuance would have been possible. As Table 2 shows, Corelli and Handel did very little to fill in the notational gaps between *forte* and *piano*. Bach used an increasingly large range of dynamic markings as time went on,[13] whilst Vivaldi used the widest range of all. Most of the dynamics added by composers to their compositions are echoes of the kind that Walther mentioned: a repeated phrase is simply played less loudly. The normal downward step is from *forte* to *piano*, but in places there are further steps from *piano* to *pianissimo*, as in the fourth movement of Handel's Trio Sonata Op. 2 No. 4. Here and there, however, the added dynamics have nothing to do with echo phrasings. In the Larghetto of Handel's Op. 2 No. 4 Sonata, for instance, the cello is asked to produce a sudden and somewhat awkward *piano* during the course of a phrase that stretches from bars 12 to 15 (Example 20). Could it be that Handel's cellist would have made a diminuendo during the previous

**Ex. 20**   Handel, Trio Sonata Op. 2 No. 4

bar? In such a passage as the one shown in Example 21, from Vivaldi's Concerto P428, the implications of a gradual dynamic change are much more clearly spelt out:

**Ex. 21**    Vivaldi, Concerto P428: Allegro

as they are in bars 76–9 of the closing chorus of Bach's St Matthew Passion.

Undoubtedly, musical notation lagged far behind practice, for despite Maffei's clear account of orchestral crescendos and diminuendos, composers did not begin to use specific signs for these effects until Mozart's day. Perhaps, like the English organist and composer Charles Avison, people felt that subtleties of interpretation are better demonstrated than explained:

> The energy and grace of Musical Expression [he wrote] is of too delicate a Nature to be fixed by words; it is a matter of taste, rather than of reasoning, and is therefore much better understood by example than by precept.[14]

## CORELLI'S SLOW MOVEMENTS: ITALIAN IMPROVISED ORNAMENTATION

Enough has already been said to suggest that musicians of the early eighteenth century fully recognised the existence of national styles of music. Certainly there were two national systems of ornamentation. The Italian one was mainly improvised, no indication being given in the notation as to where or how the ornamentation was to be applied. The French system was indicated by signs, though as we shall see, these signs still left a good deal to the player (see below, p. 58). The Italian convention enabled a sensitive player to transform a simple melodic skeleton into an intricately shaped and highly expressive melody. In 1710, the Amsterdam publisher Estienne Roger published a third edition of Corelli's Op. 5 Sonatas (he was one of the four publishers to issue the first edition in 1700). In it he printed what he claimed were Corelli's improvised embellishments – a claim that John Walsh made in the following year when he reprinted Roger's third edition.[15]

The 3/2 Adagio from the Eleventh Sonata is given in Example 22. The character of such an improvisation would undoubtedly have been very much coloured by the temperament of the player. In Example 23, taken from the Fifth Op. 5 Sonata, the Corelli ornamentation is very much plainer than the flamboyant top line, which was how the virtuoso Dubourg played it. Dubourg was a pupil of the famous violinist and teacher Geminiani, who had himself studied with Corelli.[16]

Ex. 22    Corelli, Op. 5 No. 11: Adagio

Ex. 23    Corelli, graced by Corelli and Dubourg

As often as not, the note values of the florid lines simply do not add up; there are, for instance, fourteen quavers in Dubourg's quoted bar! This is admittedly an exceptional instance, but the inference must be, nevertheless, that embellished slow movements were played quite freely. Fast movements, too, were often ornamented, though much more simply, especially in operatic arias (see below, p. 86). No examples have survived of fast-movement ornamentation in Corelli's music.

Judging from the surviving evidence of the unwritten practice of improvised ornamentation (and a surprisingly large quantity of evidence is available), certain conclusions can be drawn as to what was and what was not done. The total length of the piece seems to have been preserved, no bars being added or subtracted. The ranges of the original parts were not exceeded, nor were the harmonies significantly altered. Slow movements were ornamented much more elaborately than fast ones, and they were played somewhat freely, with a certain amount of rhythmic give and take. All instruments were treated in the same way, no distinctions being made between stringed and wind instruments. Sequential patterns and repetitions were not necessarily retained in the embellishment. Fast movements, when ornamented, were treated simply, by filling in small leaps and by preserving the metrical flow of the music.

### SOME BRIEF ANALYTICAL COMMENTS ON CORELLI'S SONATA OP. 5 NO. 11

Corelli's music is far less complex than Bach's, and there is consequently much less of an analytical nature to say. Nonetheless, figures, phrases, harmonic rhythms, cadences, tessitura and texture are, as before, important shaping ingredients that must be considered. The simple opening Adagio is articulated by cadences in bars 6 and 10, taking the music to the dominant and to the relative minor of the tonic. Interpretatively this could well be reflected by an almost imperceptible broadening at these points, taking care not to anticipate the finality of the tonic cadence in bar 16 two bars earlier, where there is also a tonic cadence. The tessitura of the violin line steadily mounts in the opening five bars; individual phrases are separated by rests, and each is higher than its predecessor. A similar ascent occurs in bars 7–10, and an even more intense one from 10 onwards. Whilst the high B of the first section (in bar 5) is not exceeded in the third (bars 10 to the end), the build-up to the B in bar 12 is far more powerful (the semitone steps in the continuo and the syncopated violin figures contribute much to this). From bar 14 the music relaxes into the final cadence. The paired semiquaver slurring suggests that Corelli had in mind a fairly firm, legato sound: the pair of slurs at the beginning of the sixth bar should be *heard* as slurs, the first note in each pair being slightly overlong (see below, p. 126). In the absence of a dynamic marking, the general level may be assumed to be *forte*, though intensity builds up from section to section, the third and last being the most powerful.

Though the ensuing Allegro is in binary form, it has elements of ternary form about it. The first half remains in the tonic; the second opens dramatically in the relative minor, moving seven bars later to G sharp minor (relatively uncharted waters at that time, outside the realm of opera!). It then goes straight back into the tonic and remains there until the final close. The phrasing is largely in groups of two and four bars. The violin line of the first four bars becomes the bass line of the next four. A sequential run of four bars follows, and after an interrupted cadence (bar 14), two bars are immediately echoed, *piano*. The phrase structure of the second half is equally obvious. There is a shortening process, in that single bar repetitions now occur (19=20; 25=26), whereas initially the unit of repetition was four bars (1–4=5–8) and then two (15–16=17–18). On the return of the tonic at bar 31, we seem to be heading for a repeat of the opening. Only the first two bars of that four-bar phrase appear, however; and while the rhythmic pattern of bars 9–12 is repeated, the figure now stretches upward to high B (bar 37), bars 37–8 being echoed by way of conclusion. The techniques are simple enough. Only by seeing the music for what it is, however, will appropriate nuances be applied to the basic *forte* – perhaps some slight decrescendo between bars 9 and 12, returning to the original level at 13; a dramatic *forte* immediately after the double bar, mirroring the key change; and from bar 34 a crescendo to 37 (after a small diminuendo in 35), possibly the peak of the movement. Finally, the basic figure suggests a bold style of articulation, with plenty of space between the quavers, and some vigorous semiquaver passagework.

# 4

## Couperin's *Huitième Ordre*

LIBRARY, UNIVERSITY OF CHESTER

> There are similar faults, I maintain, in the way that we write music and in
> the way that we write words, for the fact is that our manner of writing differs
> from our manner of delivery. As a result of this, foreigners play our music
> far less well than we do theirs. Unlike us, the Italians write their music in
> the true values that are intended. For instance, we dot quavers that follow
> each other in conjunct motion, and yet we notate them equal. Our conven-
> tion has enslaved us, and we continue to observe it.[1]

If asked to explain why French performance conventions differed from those
of other countries, the French would undoubtedly have replied that they
were much more interested in expressive subtlety than grand effect. They
would probably have added that their unwritten conventions gave the good
player the necessary freedom to be expressive. Couperin declared in the
preface to his first book of *Pièces de clavecin* (Paris, 1713), that he much
preferred when listening to music to be 'moved' rather than 'astonished',
and that as a composer he placed 'sensibilité' above 'virtuosité'. His preface
to the very first set of keyboard suites makes this very plain:

> The harpsichord is a complete instrument by virtue of its range, and sufficient
> unto itself. However, as one can neither swell nor diminish its sounds, I shall
> be always grateful to those who, by consummate skill supported by good taste,
> are able to render this instrument capable of expression. Such was the task my
> ancestors set themselves, quite apart from the fine quality of their pieces. I
> have endeavoured to perfect their discoveries, for their works still appeal to
> persons of refined taste.

French concern for *sensibilité* was manifest in several ways: in a fastidiously
detailed vocabulary of performance instructions; in a complex system of
symbol ornamentation; and above all in a rhythmic system of great subtlety,
which embraced not only the unwritten convention of *notes inégales* but also
an equally unwritten convention of rhythmic flexibility centering on the
concept of cadence.

## TEMPO AND MOOD TERMS

> All our *airs de violons* [Couperin explained], all our pieces for harpsichord, for
> viols, etc., are designed to express, and seem to seek to express some sentiment.
> And since we have not thought out any signs or characters to express our
> specific ideas, we try to make up for this by heading our pieces with such words
> as *Tendrement, Vivement*, etc., suggesting as closely as possible how we would like
> the music to be heard.[2]

Like their Italian contemporaries, French composers increasingly qualified the standard terms of tempo and mood during the early eighteenth
century. It is perhaps symptomatic of the French concern for *sensibilité* that in
the keyboard music of François Couperin particularly, the markings tend to
be less informative about speed than about mood. The movements of the
magnificent Eighth *Ordre* or Suite in B minor, for instance, are variously
headed, 'Légèrement et marqué' (Allemande), 'Gravement' (Sarabande),
'Tendrement' (Gavotte), 'Gayement' (Rondeau) and 'Légèrement, et très
lié' ('La Morinete'). This last movement serves as a reminder of the fact that
Couperin did in fact set out frequently to write character pieces – 'La
Morinete' seems to have been written as a tribute to one of the daughters of
the composer Jean-Baptiste Morin, for instance. As Couperin explained in
the preface to his first book of suites, he was often inspired to composition by
things that he had seen and heard, and even by moods: titles such as 'Le
Petit-deuil, ou les trois Veuves', and 'La Triomphante' are highly characteristic and invite the performer to emphasise the music's expressive qualities.

## RHYTHMIC CONVENTIONS: (1) 'INÉGALITÉ'

The importance of this unwritten convention has perhaps been overempha-
sised in recent times. Surprisingly perhaps, there is only the briefest reference to it in *L'art de toucher le clavecin* – surprisingly, if only because Couperin
sought in his little book to concentrate on questions of taste rather than
technique, and because the application of the *inégales* convention was so very
clearly a matter of taste. As it is, Couperin's one reference to it comes in the
passage quoted above, in which only one kind of note value is mentioned,
completely disregarding metre or tempo: as he put it, 'we dot quavers that
follow each other in conjunct motion'.[3]

Couperin's casualness here may be interpreted in one of several ways.
Certainly *L'art de toucher le clavecin* is less systematic on the subject than could
be wished; it has shortcomings in other areas as well. The convention may,
however, have been so much a part of French performance that it needed no
explanation. Or Couperin may have considered it to be such an optional
element in performance that it merited only the briefest mention. There is
perhaps some truth in all three possibilities. The *inégales* convention is

outlined in a good many French sources of the late seventeenth and early eighteenth centuries; yet no two accounts agree precisely in detail – a point that perhaps underlines the importance of individual taste in interpretation.

Inequality may be loosely summarised as follows:

(i)  The alternate lengthening and shortening of evenly written successions of conjunct notes: the longer notes are those in the stronger accentual positions (e.g. in a group of four notes that start on the beat, the first and third are longer than the second and fourth).

(ii)  The notes in question are normally *half* the length of the note representing the metric pulse, thus:

| Time signature | Note values to be made unequal |
| --- | --- |
| 3/2 | crotchet; in many cases, however, the quaver would seem to be the value to alter |
| 6/4, fast 'Common time' C, C-stroke *Alla breve* | quaver |
| 3/8, 4/8, 6/8, 9/8, 12/8 | semiquaver |

In the cases of the two most commonly used metres, 3/4 and 4/4, the convention was by no means clear-cut. In slow common time (C-stroke, C and 4/4) the value to be made unequal was normally (though not invariably) the semiquaver, not the quaver. Opinions differed most as to what to do in 3/4 time. In quick time, the quaver would seem to be the value that was altered, unless the movement was largely in semiquavers.

(iii)  The more energetic the music, the more pronounced would the inequality have been.

(iv)  The ratio between the first and second notes was normally less than 3:1, i.e. less than dotted.

(v)  Under the following circumstances, inequality was *not* to be applied: (a) when notes were slurred or dotted; (b) when the instruction 'égale' was given; (c) when the notes moved by leap; and (d) when notes were repeated.

A few examples from Couperin's B minor Suite may serve to illustrate how inequality might have been applied.

(1)  'La Raphaèle'. The texture of this piece suggests a slow 4/4. Inequality, therefore, should apply to the semiquavers.

**Ex. 24**   Couperin, *Huitième Ordre*: 'La Raphaèle'

(2) Allemande 'L'Ausoniène'. In view of the 4/8 time signature, the inequality would only apply to the semiquaver. Most of the conjunct semiquavers are slurred, however (see Example 38).

**Ex. 25**   Couperin, *Huitième Ordre*: Allemande, 'L'Ausoniène'

(3–4) Courantes I and II. As the time signature is 3/2, the values to be altered should be crotchets. Unequal crotchets are actually notated in the right hand. Even if inequality were to be applied to the quavers, only the second Courante would be affected substantially.

**Ex. 26** Couperin, *Huitième Ordre*: Courantes

(5–6) Sarabande 'L'Unique', and Gavotte. There would have been little or no opportunity for inequality here: the semiquavers at the end of the first half of the Gavotte might just possibly have been dotted if the music had been seen as a slowish 4/4 (much would have depended on the interpretation of 'tendrement').

**Ex. 27**   Couperin, *Huitième Ordre*: Sarabande, 'L'Unique'

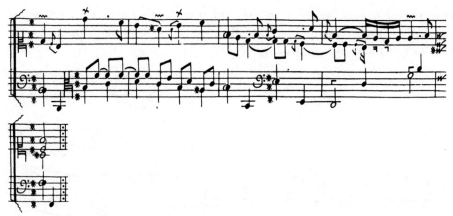

**Ex. 28**   Couperin, *Huitième Ordre*: Gavotte

(7) Rondeau. In all probability the quavers would have been made un-equal.

**Ex. 29**   Couperin, *Huitième Ordre*: Rondeau

(8) Gigue. As there are no semiquavers, no inequality would have been possible.

(9) Passacaille. The music being fairly brisk and semiquavers all but absent apart from the last eight bars, the quaver would probably have been seen as the value to alter. Perhaps the thirds in the right hand in bars 54–63 would have been played unequally. The Passacaille is full of dotted quaver/

semiquaver groups, however; care should be taken, therefore, if the following passage is played unequally, to differentiate its rhythms from the 3+1 rhythms of the dotted figures.

Ex. 30  Couperin, *Huitième Ordre*: Passacaille

(10) 'La Morinete'. No inequality could have been applied to this final movement.

Ex. 31  Couperin, *Huitième Ordre*: 'La Morinete'

The inequality convention, then, could have affected only a very small part of the B minor suite – and its application could by no means have been an automatic process.

Just how relevant the *inégales* convention would have been to non-French music has been the subject of much heated debate recently. Some scholars have argued that it should be applied to preclassical music of all nationalities and periods. The weight of evidence, however, suggests that it was exclusively French. The French-speaking Loys Bourgeois mentioned it as early as 1550 in his *Le droict chemin*. The next published account is to be found in Guillaume Nivers' *Livre d'orgue* (Paris, 1665). Between 1665 and 1760, well over forty writers and composers discussed inequality, almost all of them French. None of these suggests that the convention was anything but French. As we shall later see (p. 72 below), performers of all nationalities took liberties with written rhythms when the spirit moved. It would be misleading, however, to equate a very free, improvisatory practice with the French convention of inequality, which was based on broadly formulated principles that were applied from the beginning to the end of a piece and not simply wherever the player felt moved to apply them!

### RHYTHMIC CONVENTIONS: (II) 'CADENCE ET MÉSURE': RHYTHMIC FLEXIBILITY AND PHRASING

Couperin argued that one of the most important qualities which distinguished an expressive performance from a routine one was rhythmic flexibility, a quality that called for a sensitivity to cadence. 'I find [he wrote] that we confuse "la mesure" with what is called "cadence". "Mesure" defines the quantity and the equality of time; "cadence" is properly the spirit and the soul that must be joined to it [viz. "Mesure"].' Couperin believed that cadence depended above all on the *cessation* and *suspension* of sounds – in other words, the way in which notes are released and attacked. He evidently attached the greatest importance to this, for it is the very first purely interpretative advice that he gives in *L'art de toucher le clavecin*, following a survey of basic manual techniques.[4] The *cessation*, or *aspiration*, has the effect of placing an accent on the following note. Couperin indicates the aspiration by the familiar dash, the note in question being almost invariably on the upbeat. The *suspension* is not the modern form of tied note, but a momentary delay before a note is played. It almost invariably falls on the downbeat. Couperin's interpretation of the *aspiration* and *suspension* given in his table of performance signs is shown in Example 32; he would undoubtedly have explained that the precise length of the delay should be a matter of 'taste' rather than of strict 'mesure':

A combination of *aspiration* and *suspension* enhances the feeling of accentuation, as in, for instance, bar 11 of 'Les Laurentines' [*Troisième Ordre*]. While Couperin continued to use the *aspiration* sign throughout his twenty-seven

**Ex. 32**  Couperin's 'aspiration' and 'suspension'

keyboard suites, he dropped the *suspension* after the second book, perhaps on the grounds that the player should instinctively feel where the delay is appropriate. At the same time he began to use the comma with a similar but not identical purpose. In effect, Couperin's commas are the first notation signs to show that composers of the high baroque wished their music to be articulated in long phrases as well as short *figurae*. The point is worth making, as so much emphasis has recently been placed on the importance of *figurae*, and on parallels between verbal and musical 'rhetoric'. The contexts in which Couperin used the comma should be closely studied, as should Couperin's own carefully worded description in the preface to the *Troisième Livre*, of how the comma was to be played:

> A new sign will be found, which appears thus,'; it is used to mark the ending of phrases or of our *phrases harmoniques* [harmonic sentences], and to indicate a slight break at the end of a phrase before the following one. Generally speaking this is almost imperceptible, although when the Little Silence is not observed, persons of taste feel that something is lacking in the performance: in a word, it is the difference between those who read everything straight through, and those who pause at the full stops and commas. These silences must make themselves felt without altering the beat.

Couperin's concept of the 'harmonic sentence' is an apt reminder that musical phrases are indeed defined by their harmonic structure; that imperfect and interrupted cadences can have the effect of a musical comma, whilst perfect cadences can have the effect of a full stop. It is no accident, then, that many of Couperin's articulating commas occur at such cadence points (see Example 33).

Couperin also uses commas in places that are less obvious: in 'Les Fauvettes Plaintives', for instance, he is obviously aiming at a special effect (Example 34). Such musical punctuation is the stuff of music, no matter what the period or the nationality. It would be surprising, then, if Couperin's contemporaries abroad were not as sensitive as he in this respect.

**Ex. 33**  Couperin's comma

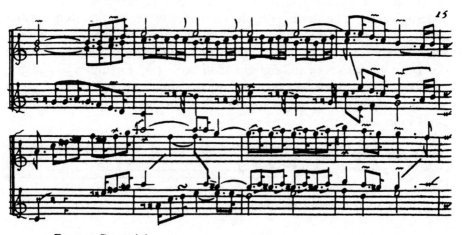

**Ex. 34**  Couperin's comma

## COUPERIN'S FINGERING AS EVIDENCE OF PHRASING AND ARTICULATION

Couperin was the first major composer to examine this aspect of keyboard performance. Despite a certain lack of system, his remarks do have the very real virtue of relating to actual music – specifically, to the music of the first two books of *Pièces de clavecin*. Many of the examples have the purpose of ensuring a true legato; indeed, Couperin almost seems to be suggesting that the technique of changing fingers on a sustained note (as, for instance, the right hand in bar 22 of the Allemande, 'L'Ausoniène', in the Eighth Suite) was unknown before his time. He certainly claims originality for the legato paired third fingerings in bars 55–8 of the Passacaille (Example 35; see also his discussion in *L'art*, 'Endroits de mon second livre').

**Ex. 35**   Couperin's fingering of thirds

He is, moreover, the first to recognise the awkwardness of the old paired fingerings in keys that call for more than two accidentals. Many of his fingerings seem to be alerting the player, in fact, to a departure from normal practice towards a new, legato style of articulation; occasionally he goes to extraordinary lengths to secure legato, as in the Gigue of the Eighth *Ordre* (left hand in bars 11–13 and right hand in bars 34–9, Examples 36 and 37). In such places as these the sounding note has almost disappeared before the next one is played; the fingering, then, is rather more psychological than aural in its effect.

**Ex. 36**   Couperin's legato fingering

**Ex. 37**   Couperin's legato fingering

But if Couperin insisted on a true legato whenever the notation demanded (particularly by slurring), this is not to suggest that he had a continuous legato as his ideal. In this respect, the fingerings of the Allemande, 'L'Ausoniène', deserve the closest attention (see Example 38).

**Ex. 38**   Couperin's fingering of 'L'Ausoniène'

Fingered upbeat to downbeat patterns that are unslurred (e.g. bars 5–6, 7–8, 10–11 and 31–2) show unarguably a break between upbeat and downbeat similar to the kind of articulation we have already met in the Bach Prelude (see above, p. 8). On the other hand, slurred crossbeats are carefully fingered to ensure continuity of sounds, as in bars 1–2 and 5. Many of the tied notes that are fingered (e.g. bars 14–15) have to be lifted before the next notes are sounded as indeed they do in the Bach prelude. Where Couperin wishes otherwise, he carefully marks in the fingering, as in bars 22–3 and 40–1.

A good deal of ink has been spilt on the implications for articulation of paired fingerings in conjunct motion: Bach, it will be remembered, taught Wilhelm Friedemann the technique in a simple C major *Applicatio* (p. 9 above). Although Couperin, like Bach, used our modern thumbs-under method a good deal, vestiges of the paired system remain, even in an awkward key like B minor. Interestingly, though, he saw no incongruity in slurring extended groups of notes together, as in bars 17 and 31 above. According to French conventions, such slurs indicated not only a total legato but a total equality of note values: there can be no question of *inégalité* at such points. Evidently, then, it is incorrect to argue, as certain authorities have recently done, that paired fingerings have any influence on phrasing or articulation.

Two further points emerge from the fingering in 'L'Ausoniéne'. Slurs are emphasised in several places by detaching the immediately preceding notes. Bar 3 is an interesting case in point where the fingering in the first half of the bar differs from that of the second, although the figures are similar. The first figure could be played legato; the second, however, must be articulated by a break between C sharp and B. Similar breaks are unavoidable in bars 7 and 20. The second point concerns the articulation of inner parts. Here again, the 'L'Ausoniéne' fingering of bars 11, 23 and 44 suggests a modest degree of detachment, special fingerings being devised when a true legato is required, as in bars 41–3.

FRENCH SYMBOL ORNAMENTS

In theory at least, symbol ornaments should cause the player no difficulty. Many French composers went to the trouble of publishing ornaments tables in which the signs were realised in conventional notation,[5] yet no aspect of performance has been so controversial. The most recent book on the subject covers some 600 pages, and it refers to some 250 other books and articles![6]

Broadly speaking, early eighteenth-century ornament symbols are of six kinds: trills, single-note (appoggiatura-type) ornaments, mordents, turns, coulés and arpeggios. When interpreting an ornament, six questions need to be asked. On what note should the ornament begin? Should it start before, on or after the beat? How fast should it be played? How long should it go on? Should the notes of the ornament be diatonic, or should accidentals be introduced in particular circumstances? And (in the case of the trill) how should it end?

> I am always astonished [Couperin wrote] after the pains I have taken to indicate the appropriate ornaments (I have given a fairly intelligible explanation of these under separate cover in a special *Method* known as *L'Art de toucher le clavecin*) to hear persons who have learnt my pieces without heeding my instructions. Such negligence is unpardonable, the more so as ornamentation is no arbitrary matter to be put in as one pleases. I therefore declare that my

pieces must be performed just as I have written them, and that they will never make much of an impression on persons of real taste, as long as all that I have marked is not observed to the letter, without adding or taking away anything.[7]

Let us then see how much can be learned about ornamentation from *L'art de toucher le clavecin* (referred to hereafter as *L'adet*) and from the ornament table which Couperin supplied at the end of his first book of *Pièces de clavecin* (hereafter *Pdec*).

### The trill [*tremblement*]

Couperin supplied six examples of trills in the *Pdec* table (these are shown in Example 39).

**Ex. 39**  Couperin's trills

Typically there are no speed or mood markings, nor are the examples placed in any kind of context. The unexplained realisations in the table leave all sorts of questions unanswered. Should the trill begin on, after or before the beat? How is the irrational notation to be interpreted (there are, for instance, nine semiquavers to the first minim of the 'tremblement continu')? Should all the notes within the trill be played at the same speed? Should the speed of the trill relate to the established tempo? How exactly should the tremblements end in the versions described as 'appuyé', 'fermé' and 'ouvert'? And, although the trill is always interpreted as beginning on the upper note, there are, as we shall see, arguments against making this an absolute rule. Some of the answers are given in *L'adet*, but by no means all. 'Whatever the note is, over which a tremblement is marked [Couperin writes] one must always begin on the tone or semitone above it.' This seems clear enough. But what if consecutives are produced, as in bar 21 of the Eighth *Ordre*'s Seconde Courante (Example 40)?

**Ex. 40**    Couperin, *Huitième Ordre*: Seconde Courante (bars 17–25)

Whether such a solecism would have been countenanced is uncertain, though in such an obvious context the likely answer must surely be no. Consecutive fifths, after all, could easily be avoided by beginning the trill on the main note, or by delaying the start fractionally. The problem of consecutives, however, is never discussed, either by Couperin or anyone else.

The question of whether to begin the trill before, on, or after the beat is also left entirely open. Couperin does not discuss the matter in *L'adet*, and his notated examples of the 'Tremblement lié sans être appuyé' and the 'Tremblement détaché' are perhaps deliberately ambiguous.

In his discussion of long trills, Couperin makes it quite clear that the player must decide (1) how long the upper note is to be held at the beginning of the trill (the *L'adet* example shows that this could be up to half the value of the main note); (2) how long the actual trill is to last; (3) how fast it is to be played (Couperin does, however, say that long trills are to begin slowly and accelerate); and, (4) how it is to be terminated. A trill, Couperin suggests, may even end in an aspiration (see above, p. 54). Obviously, then, ornament tables and explanations such as those that Couperin printed in the *Pdec* can show only the general shape of an ornament, not its precise detail. Nor should we assume that eighteenth-century players would have aimed at consistency of realisation throughout a piece: the musical context in which the ornament is placed must affect the interpretation; good taste – the *bon goût* of the performer – must be the final arbiter. Either of the right-hand trills in the second bar of *La Raphaèle*, for instance, may be stopped on the second quaver beat, or continued into the succeeding note (see above, Example 24); the trill in bar 10 of the Seconde Courante may be carried through into the following bar or stopped at any point during the dotted minim, as the player sees fit (see above, Example 26).

### The *pincé* [*mordent*]

Similar decisions are left to the performer in interpreting the mordent [*pincé*] (see Example 41). All the examples in the *Pdec* table show the ornament starting on the main note. Very occasionally an open consecutive may occur

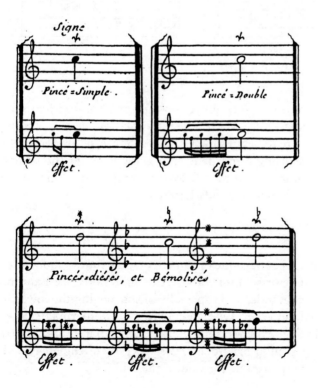

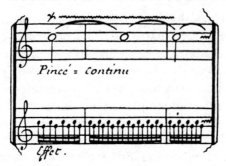

**Ex. 41**   Couperin's mordent

if this is done, though there are none in the Eighth *Ordre*. A possible solution then might be to begin the ornament on the lower note, as indeed is the case when the mordent is incorporated into the *port de voix* (see Example 42).

**Ex. 42**   Couperin's *port de voix*

There is, however, no explicit comment on this problem in either the *Pdec* or *L'adet*, or for that matter elsewhere. By extrapolation we may assume that extended mordents are to begin slowly and accelerate, as are long trills. The main problem in realising a mordent is to know whether the second note should sound a semitone or a tone below the main note. Once again, the player is left to decide what sounds best.

### The turn

Like the *Pdec* table, most baroque ornaments tables show a four-note figure beginning on the tone or semitone above the main note (see Example 43). The problem of accidentals, and especially of sharpening the lower note, is completely ignored, however. Oddly enough, too, Couperin fails to explain the much used double ornament in which a turn is placed above a trill. To judge from roughly similar ornaments, described by d'Anglebert and Muffat, the turn is to be placed at the end of the trill.

**Ex. 43**  Couperin's turn

*Appoggiatura-type single-note ornaments*

These are more difficult to interpret than any other kind of ornament, though they are superficially the simplest. Couperin illustrates three kinds, as shown in Example 44: the first comes either as a melodic ornament (the *port de voix coulé*), or as a harmonic ornament, filling in the space between notes sounding a third apart (the *tierce coulée*).

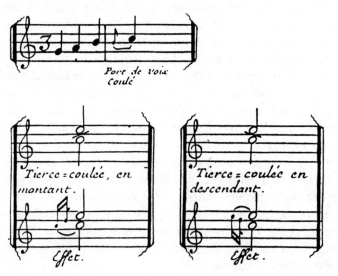

**Ex. 44**  Couperin's *port de voix* and *tierce coulée*

Couperin almost always uses the small note for the melodic *coulé*, whereas other composers (and especially Bach) also use the dash, which Couperin reserves for the *tierce coulée*. Example 45 shows the old and the new manner of fingering; Couperin's overriding concern was to connect the *note perdue* (i.e. the actual grace note) to its immediate predecessor in as legato a manner as possible, as he explained in *L'adet*:

*Reasons for preferring the new manner of fingering 'ports de voix'*

As the fingers marked 3 in the *troisième progrès*, and 4 in the *quatrième progrès* are forced to release the quaver marked x in order to repeat the little *note perdue*, there is less *liaison* [than in the modern style fingerings].

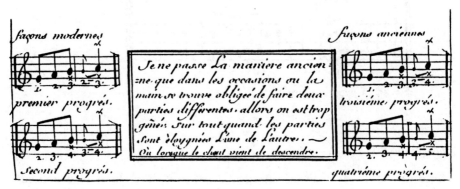

Ex. 45    Couperin's old and new fingerings of the *port de voix*

The only other point that Couperin makes about single grace-note ornaments in *L'adet* is that the *note perdue* must be 'struck with the harmony: that is to say, at the moment that the main note to which it is attached should be played'. (As we have already seen there is good reason to question even this apparently unambiguous instruction.) But what about the *length* of the grace notes? Couperin supplies realisations of the *tierces coulées*, to be sure, which seem to suggest that the grace note should be played quite fast: the preliminary grace note in the *port de voix simple* is one quarter of the length of the main note, and that of the *port de voix double*, a sixth. 'Generally speaking [he writes at the beginning of the section on ornamentation] it is the value of the [main] note which determines the length of the *pincé double*, the *port de voix double* and the *tremblement*.' But how long should the melodic *port de voix coulé* actually be – a quarter, a sixth, or even perhaps half the value of the main note? And should it relate to the speed and 'affect' of the piece? Perhaps Couperin was being deliberately vague. Certainly no consensus emerges from a study of other ornaments tables. The upward or downward appoggiatura takes half the value of the main note in d'Anglebert's table, but only a quarter of the value in Muffat's. (See Example 46.)[8]

Once again it seems that the player was left to make the ultimate decision, a decision that would undoubtedly have been affected by the harmonic, rhythmic, melodic and textural context in which the ornament was placed. It could be that the jagged rhythms of 'La Raphaèle' suggest a very crisp, almost acciaccatura style of grace note at the beginning of the second bar (see Example 24 above); certainly a rapid grace-note G sharp would go well with the broken chord figuration of that first beat. On the other hand the F sharp appoggiatura, in bar 4, might well be held rather longer, in order to

**Ex. 46**   The appoggiatura: d'Anglebert and Muffat compared

emphasise the F sharp/E dissonance. In this case, the interpretation would be influenced by both harmonic and rhythmic considerations. Longer grace notes would suit the smoother, more flowing character of the first Courante; the value might well be half that of the main note in the second bar (cf. Example 26 above).

Grace notes that are attached to dotted notes can be particularly difficult to interpret. While post-baroque authors mention the possibility of the grace note taking two-thirds of the main value (see below, p. 145) there is little evidence that such an interpretation was common in earlier times. Frederick Neumann argues, indeed, that an ornament would have been written out in normal notation whenever such an extended appoggiatura was required. In the tenth bar of the Sarabande 'L'Unique', then, the right-hand A (sharp) would probably have been no longer than a quaver (Example 27 above). As most single-note graces form a dissonance that resolves into a consonance, a quaver would in this case be preferable to a semiquaver, since it would allow more time for the impact of the dissonance to be felt.

The *coulé* also occurs occasionally, as in Example 47, as two equal quavers (or semiquavers) joined together by a slur, the second note having a dot above it and thus *plus appuyée* [more leaned on]. The explanation is again imprecise, though the implication seems to be that there is a slight inequality between the two notes, the first being the shorter.

**Ex. 47**   Couperin's dotted *coulés*

*Other ornaments*

As far as Couperin is concerned, the only other significant ornament is the *arpègement*. A small hook added to the bottom of the sign indicates that the chord is to be spread upwards. Similarly, an upper hook indicates a downward spread. (See Example 48.)

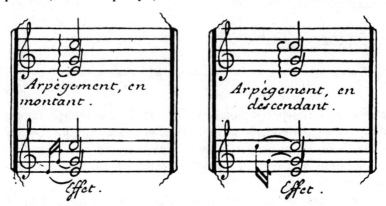

**Ex. 48**   Couperin's *arpègements*

### OVERDOTTING

Almost every movement of the Eighth *Ordre* contains some irrational notation in which the rhythmic values do not add up. Such notation represents the surface of a largely hidden (because largely improvised) tradition of rhythmic alteration that can be traced back well into the sixteenth century. Alteration of two kinds can be identified: the exaggeration of already dotted rhythms (a practice which may for convenience be described as 'overdotting'), and the arbitrary dotting of evenly written successions of notes. This second form of rhythmic alteration is not to be confused with the more systematic French tradition of inequality discussed above (p. 46), for to judge from the surviving evidence, it was not consistently applied from beginning to end of a piece, nor did the alteration relate to its metre. The process rather was one of 'jazzing up' selected phrases by dotting them. The passage from Purcell's *A Choice Collection of Lessons* (London, 1696) given in Example 49, for instance, occurs in both dotted and undotted forms in contemporary sources. In this particular case the variations are actually written down; an imaginative player, however, would have had no difficulty in improvising them.

    There are hundreds of such variations in baroque sources. Indeed, this kind of informal inequality can be traced right back to Santa Maria's *Arte de tañer fantasia* (Valladolid, 1565) and beyond! As we have seen, Couperin expected the performer to adhere strictly to what was written. Whether his French

**Ex. 49**   Purcell, Suite in G: Allemande

contemporaries would have allowed the performer some freedom in this matter is a moot point. There is, however, a good deal of evidence to show that the French liked crisp dotted rhythms. Indeed, the French composers of Lully's generation seem to have taken care to write out overdotted rhythms whenever they wanted them, as in Example 50 and 51.

**Ex. 50**   Double dotting: André Raison, Second Kyrie

**Ex. 51**   Double dotting: Lully, Overture to *Amadis*

The double dot and its tied equivalent disappeared between 1700 and 1750, however, perhaps because there was an unwritten convention of overdotting and because the business of writing out overdotted rhythms was cumbersome and time-consuming. Couperin goes so far as to use a kind of shorthand notation, in which the fastest notes have four and even five beams in spite of the fact that they are associated with simple dotted rhythms. The left-hand figure in the second bar of the Sarabande 'L 'Unique' is notated to show that the *tirade* figure should be played at the last possible moment before the barline (see Example 27 above). The three-note figures in the Vivement sections are in a sense dotted, the four-beamed notes suggesting a delayed and extremely rapid performance. In view of his expressed concern that the player should observe the notation meticulously, Couperin probably indicated every passage that was to be overdotted, though of this we cannot be certain. Later theorists – notably J. J. Quantz and C. P. E. Bach – suggested that the player should overdot a good deal. Quantz, for instance, advised that 3+1 rhythms such as dotted quaver/semiquaver should be played crisply, the short note being somewhat shorter than written, the long one longer. He also discussed the principle of 'synchronisation', whereby dotted rhythms were aligned to the shortest values of the concurrent parts, as in Example 52.

**Ex. 52**   Quantz's dotted rhythms

In no sense, however, should the overdotting convention be turned into a rule. The evidence for its existence is shadowy and somewhat contradictory. Quantz implied that only French music should be overdotted; Bach did not refer to national styles at all. Quantz treated slow and fast music similarly, while Bach recommended that the dotting should be less marked in slow and expressive music. If two authors working for the same patron and publishing their books within a year of each other could not agree, is it likely that there could have been any very precise international convention of overdotting?

The context in which overdotting is most often applied nowadays is the *Ouvertüre* or 'French overture', so called because it commonly formed the opening movement of French opera and ballet. Lully is credited as the originator of the form. D'Anglebert published three of Lully's overtures transcribed for solo harpsichord in his 1689 *Pièces de clavecin*; in all three the original note values are preserved, no hint being given of any double dotting convention. And since, as we have seen, Lully did use double dots here and there, the assumption must be that the note values should be played as they are written, with perhaps some very modest exaggeration of dotted crotchet/quaver rhythms. However, as there are no such overtures by Couperin, further discussion of the overdotting of French overtures will be postponed to the chapter in which we study one of Bach's grandest compositions of the kind (see p. 72 below). As we shall see, there are no easy solutions to the problem.[9]

## POSTSCRIPT: NATIONAL STYLES OF HARPSICHORD

Modern makers have now realised that attempts to 'improve' the harpsichord by such refinements as metal frames, pedal stop-change mechanisms and adjustable jacks are futile, for they simply impair the sound of the instrument, interfere with its sensitivity of touch and encourage a kaleidoscopic (and thus anachronistic) use of tone colour. Players have discovered, too, that the special qualities of, say, a French instrument of Couperin's day, by the contemporary Blanchet family, are particularly well suited to French music of the period, and that the sound is very different to that of an English Shudi. The establishment of 'working' collections of keyboard instruments, such as the superb Russell collection in Edinburgh, has done a great deal to educate makers and players in these subtle matters.[10]

Words are quite inadequate, of course, to describe the fine distinctions of tonal quality that we are dealing with here. Nevertheless the *New Grove* comparisons of Flemish, French and English instruments may be found helpful. The French instrument of Couperin's day has no more than three registers: two at eight foot pitch and one at four, all quilled, plus a manual coupler and a buff. It has a smoothness and sweetness of tone that is very different to the 'direct, punchy' sound of the seventeenth-century Flemish harpsichord from which it developed. English instruments produce a powerful and rich sound, though they are no larger in size than French ones: *New Grove* likens the French tutti to a baroque wind ensemble, and the English tutti to a brass band! Italian instruments, by comparison, produce a shallow and highly explosive sound. Like Italian organs, Italian harpsichords changed little from the middle of the seventeenth century, when the $2\times8'$ layout became standard. They are very lightly built and their dimensions are small.

Frustratingly little is known about the harpsichords that either Bach or Domenico Scarlatti would have used. Few German instruments have survived, and they conform to no one design. The German maker Hieronymous Albrecht Haas approached design from the standpoint of an organ builder, adding 16' and 2' registers to the standard 8' and 4' pitches and even going so far as to produce a three-manual instrument! Whether Bach knew his work is not known. He would have come across the work of Gottfried Silbermann, to be sure, but alas no instrument by this maker has yet been positively identified. As to instruments that Scarlatti would have used, the one fact that is beyond dispute is that they were of modest size, having no more than two 8' stops and possibly one at 4' pitch.[11]

# 5

## Bach's *Ouvertüre* in D BWV 1068

THE DANCE SUITE AND NATIONAL STYLES

The ensemble suite, of which Bach's D major *Ouvertüre* is a particularly fine example, originated in the second half of the seventeenth century, when the idea caught on in France of putting together sequences of dance tunes from contemporary ballet and opera, particularly those of Lully. Bach may possibly have come across Lully's music first in d'Anglebert's *Pièces de clavecin* of 1689, the ornaments table of which he copied out for his own use (see above, p. 64). He may well have known, too, some of François Couperin's ensemble suites, for he is attributed with the transcription for organ of a trio from Couperin's *Les nations* (Paris, 1726) – the so-called 'Aria' in F BWV 587. He probably knew a good many French keyboard suites, too, especially those of Dieupart, which he copied out in their entirety. Bach was probably most indebted, however, to his elder German contemporaries, notably Georg Muffat, J. C. F. Fischer and Adam Reinken, all of whom had composed and published suites of ensemble dances after the French manner. Dietrich Becker was the first German to publish ensemble suites of his own that conformed to the allemande, courante, sarabande, gigue pattern: these date from 1668. J. S. Kusser was the first German to acknowledge French influence, entitling his collection *Composition de musique suivant la méthode françoise, contenant 6 ouvertures de théâtre accompagnées de plusieurs airs* (Paris, 1682). Kusser studied with Lully from 1674 to 1682. Johann Mattheson especially admired the discipline that Kusser inspired in his orchestra, following the example of his master. As we have already seen (p. 25 above), Muffat, too, had studied with Lully (1663–9). He published some fifteen sets of ensemble suites between 1695 and 1698, together with useful instructions as to how to play them in the French style. During the next forty years or so a veritable flood of German ensemble suites (*Ouvertüres* as they were commonly called) followed – Telemann alone had composed some two hundred by 1718, and by the time he died more than a thousand!

So evident is the French influence in the development of the German

ensemble suite that there is a real danger of overlooking the important part
that the Italians also played in its development. Muffat's first published
collection, after all, was a set of 'chamber' and 'church' suites with the
Italian title *Armonico tributo*. Immediately before this, Muffat had been in
Rome with Corelli, half of whose five sets of trio and solo sonatas (Opp. 1–5,
1681–1700) are dance suites, or, as he called them, 'Sonate da camera'.

The dual nationality of the suite needs to be emphasised, since it is all too
easy to assume that a collection of dances by a German composer must be
French in style, and that its movements should all be played in the French
manner – especially if the wording of the title is French. This is to ignore the
tendency of composers (and especially Bach) to borrow from both the
French and Italian idioms. The point is not entirely academic. If indeed
Couperin was correct in asserting that nonFrench music should be played as
it is written, but French music be subject to the unwritten convention of
*inégalité* (*L'art de toucher*, p. 23), then we have to decide whether German
music in an ostensibly French style should be played in the French manner.
Muffat very obviously thought that it should, for he published a long preface
on the subject in his 1695 *Florilegium Primum*. The question is at its most acute
in Bach's own music. The Allemande of the First French Suite, for instance,
has the complex rhythm and texture of a Dieupart allemande. Should
*inégalité* be applied to this allemande but not to that of the Sixth French Suite,
which has an undeniably Italianate directness of expression? (see Example
53).

**Ex. 53**  French and Italian styles: the allemandes of Bach's French Suites Nos. 1
and 3

**Ex. 54**    French and Italian styles: the courantes of Bach's French Suites Nos. 1
and 2

The Courantes from the First and Second French Suites are similarly
contrasted. Should the quavers of the first Courante be played unevenly?
(see Example 54).

The French and Italian flavours are easy enough to detect here. But what of
those very many baroque dance movements that speak Italian with a French
accent and vice versa? Can the allemandes from Bach's so-called 'English'
Suites be so neatly pigeonholed? And what about all those complex dances in
the partitas, many of which tread wholly new ground?

As far as the D major ensemble *Ouvertüre* BWV 1068 is concerned, only the
first movement is unequivocally French. The second owes a good deal to the
Italian concerto slow movement. The melodic line has the quality of an
improvisation upon a simple melody (see above, p. 41). It is underpinned,
moreover, by a striding bass very much in the Italian manner. The four
dances that follow all have tremendous rhythmic energy and a simplicity of
texture that is far removed from the French tradition.

### TEMPO, INEQUALITY AND OVERDOTTING

The opening movement, however, is unarguably what soon came to be
known as a French overture. It comprises two contrasting textures: a sonor-
ous, richly harmonic and highly dotted introduction and a dance-like, fugal
sequel. In this particular case the movement is rounded off with more
material based on the opening section. It presents the player with two
interpretative problems: *inégalité* and overdotting.

As we have already seen (p. 46 above), the note values to which *inégalité* is applied will depend on the time signature of the movement, and, especially in the case of the crotchet metres, the speed at which the music is taken. As Bach clearly marks the central section 'vite', supporting this with the alla breve time signature '2', inequality would apply to quavers rather than semiquavers. However, since there are almost no conjunct quavers, there can be no improvised inequality.

The problem with the outer sections is that Bach characteristically fails to give a speed marking. At a slow four beats to the bar inequality could well be applied to the semiquaver. At a faster speed there can be no question of inequality, as Bach has already dotted all the quaver figures. How, then, is the appropriate speed to be determined? The following metronome markings of recorded performances show just how widely modern conductors differ on this matter (the unit measured is the crotchet): Maazel, 33; Harnoncourt, 54; Pinnock, 72; Kuijken, 66.

Such descriptions of the French overture as are to be found in contemporary dictionaries suggest that there was a gradual slowing down as the eighteenth century progressed. The two earliest authorities – Mattheson (1713) and Walther (1732) – both describe the French Overture as 'fresh' and 'joyful' ['ein frisches, ermunterndes und auch zugleich *elevirtes* Wesen']. In his compendious and slightly later *Der vollkommene Capellmeister* of 1739, Mattheson introduces the ambiguous term *Edelmuth* [nobility]. By 1752 Quantz is using such words as *prächtig* and *gravitätisch* [imposing and solemn]. Long after the French overture had ceased to be a living form, Jean-Jacques Rousseau simply and prosaically described it as 'a slow piece marked Grave' (*Dictionnaire*, Paris, 1768).[1] Lully, the originator of the form, used no speed markings at all; his time signatures commonly suggest two rather than four in the bar. Handel and Bach, too, rarely indicated the speeds of the outer sections. However, Handel's few initial markings suggest a moderate rather than an extreme slowness – larghetto and even andante, rather than largo or adagio. In all probability, then, extremes are to be avoided.

The second interpretative puzzle concerns the practice of double dotting or, as it has more recently come to be known, overdotting. There is a theory that dotted rhythms and *tirades* are to be made as dotted as possible in French overtures and other pieces in that style: for instance, the D major Fugue from the first book of the '48', the 'St Anne' Organ Prelude in E flat major. The problem is to know whether or not an unwritten performance convention *did* exist. The double dot was certainly known, for André Raison used it in some of his organ music. And although Lully does not appear to have written double dotted notes, he nonetheless used ties to produce rhythms that are in effect double dotted. An example of this (admittedly a rare one) is to be found in the overture to *Amadis* – in the penultimate bar of the first section

(Example 55): the placing of the tied figure here is exceptional, for most of Lully's dotted ties cross from the weak beat to the strong:

**Ex. 55**  Lully, Overture to *Amadis*

The very fact that Lully took the trouble to spell out the overdotted rhythms at this point suggests that the dotted crotchet/quaver rhythms of the previous bars should be played as written. Whether this is a valid inference can only be a matter of opinion. The very absence of any discussion of overdotting by contemporary authorities has been used as an argument for interpreting the notation literally.[2]

Handel and Bach used the tied form of the double dot extensively, though never the double dot, which only came into general use after 1750. As is the case in Lully's music, practically all these double dottings begin on the upbeat and tie across to the downbeat, never vice versa. A comparison of the first and second violin lines in bars 6–7 of the *Ouvertüre* (see Example 56) will

**Ex. 56**  Dotting in Bach's *Ouvertüre* BWV 1068

make this clear. The second violin's A is tied (in bars 6–7) to give a duration that is equivalent to a double dotted crotchet. In the first violin line of bar 7, however, the crotchet is dotted (not double dotted) to combine with the succeeding quaver D.

It is difficult to believe that simple dotted crotchet/quaver rhythms from downbeat to upbeat, of the kind to be found in bars 7–9, would not instinctively have been overdotted, if only to synchronise with the concurrent semiquavers. Both Quantz and C. P. E. Bach make a general recommendation (without referring specifically to the French Overture) that dotted rhythms should be synchronised with concurrent parts (see above, p. 68). There are also late eighteenth-century transcriptions of Handel Overtures which double dot and synchronise Handel's original 3+1 rhythms. The snag is, however, that all these sources of evidence are post-baroque, and they may well represent a decadent tradition. One thing is certain, however: if overdotting was an accepted performance convention during the high baroque, ensembles could only have observed a very uncomplicated version of it. No orchestral parts of Bach's day contain any markings to suggest that overdotting was ever discussed during rehearsal. In all likelihood, therefore, overdotting would normally have been confined to the dotted crotchet/quaver figure and applied consistently from start to finish.

Scalic groups of three or more upbeat semiquavers or demisemiquavers – known as *tirades* – are to be found in many French overtures (see Example 57). These, too, involve the idea of overdotting. According to Quantz and C. P. E. Bach, such groups should be played 'at the end of time' – i.e. as quickly as possible.

**Ex. 57**   C. P. E. Bach's *tirades*

We have already come across *tirade*-like figures in Couperin's Eighth *Ordre*, irrational notation being used to suggest rapid execution. There are many such passages in the music of Handel and Bach: one, the third bar of Bach's D major Fugue from Book 1 of the '48', is shown in Example 58.

**Ex. 58**   J. S. Bach, Fugue in D Major BWV 874

**Ex. 59**   J. S. Bach, *Ouvertüre* BWV 1066: O'Donnell's interpretation of Bach

Often the difficulty is to decide what is a *tirade* and what is not. At first sight, for instance, the semiquaver figure in the C major *Ouvertüre* marked 'x' in Example 59 might seem to be a candidate for speeding up. That, indeed, is what John O'Donnell proposes, for he sees in the music two separate figures, an implied *tirade* and the first violin's semiquaver group in bar 1. The first figure, he argues, needs interpretation, the second must be played as written. It would surely be difficult, however, if not impossible, to get an ensemble to modify the written notes in such a complex way!

The first version of Bach's French Overture BWV 831a (*c.* 1733), would also seem to contain potential *tirades*. Indeed, Bach himself wrote it out that way in the published *Clavierübung II* version of 1735 (see Example 60). Could it be that the published version represents a realisation of the C minor version as it would actually have sounded in performance? But why then are some of the *tirade* figures in the first C minor version notated as semiquavers and others as demisemiquavers? Why, too, in a second copy of the C minor version in the hand of Bach's pupil J. G. Preller (*c.* 1735) are ornaments placed over some of the semiquaver *tirade* figures, though not over the demisemiquaver ones? If these semiquaver figures are played 'at the end of

**Ex. 60**   J. S. Bach, *Ouvertüre* BWV 831 and 831a

time', Preller's ornaments are totally unmanageable! In this case, then, only those figures that are notated in the shortest note values (normally demi-semiquavers) can possibly have been played as *tirades*.

In the *Ouvertüre* BWV 1068, then, the initial section of the first movement should probably be taken at a moderate tempo – a 4/4 andante with the crotchet equal to something between 60 and 80. The semiquaver figures (in the first two bars, for instance), should on no account be turned into *tirades*, as some conductors have recently attempted to do. Only the dotted crotchet/quaver figures should be overdotted. The demisemiquaver *tirades* may, however, be very effectively played 'at the end of time', each note being separately bowed.

### BOWING

Of the interpretative problems that remain to be discussed in connection with BWV 1068, the most substantial is undoubtedly the bowing. Although Bach never set his ideas about string playing down on paper in the way that Muffat did, the care with which he marked up much of his string music is highly informative. A good deal has already been said about the ways in which the rule of the downbow would have been applied (see above, p. 26). Bach's slurrings in his most carefully prepared scores and sets of parts are entirely consistent with Muffat's broader Italian manner of bowing, and they suggest that the players would have respected the markings. The earliest source of BWV 1068 is a mixed set of parts (there is no autograph score or printed edition). The first violin parts of the Bourrée and Gigue are autograph, as is the continuo part. The other parts are in various contempor-ary hands. The autograph sections of the first violin part are carefully and consistently slurred throughout. There is no question here of markings being placed over only the early appearances of the main figures (as is the case, for instance, in the last movement of Cantata BWV 129). The nonautograph sections of the first violin part are almost as carefully marked, although one or two slurs (especially in the second half of Gavotte II) are lacking. Given Bach's evident involvement in the preparation of parts, and given, too, the apparent accuracy of the secondary parts, alterations and additions should be kept to the minimum. Above all, editions such as the late nineteenth-century one by Peters quoted in Example 61 are to be avoided at all costs.

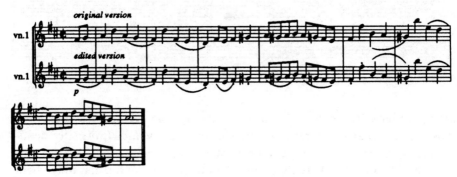

**Ex. 61**    Romantic bowings: the Bourrée of J. S. Bach's *Ouvertüre* BWV 1068

Throughout the *Ouvertüre* the player has, in fact, to make remarkably few bowing decisions. All boil down to whether to retake a bow or to play the music as it comes, there being no question of adjusting or adding to the slurring. A summary of the places where the first violinist needs to make such decisions may serve to illustrate this.

*First movement, first and third sections*
Bars 7–8 and 117: the last two notes in each case are best taken in separate upbows (see *craquer*, p. 26 above). Bars 10, 20 and 23: the second sounding note in each case may be taken in an upbow; alternatively the third beat of the previous bar may in each case be taken in a separate downbow.
*First movement, central section*. In all probability the repeated quaver/semiquaver/semiquaver figures would have been taken as they come in such places as bars 32–36, since the bowing comes out right in alternate patterns. Here and there, however, a bow has to be retaken: the semiquaver figures in bars 28–30 will begin on the upbow unless the last quaver of bar 27 is retaken as an upbow. Throughout this central section, however, the player could conceivably bow the quaver/semiquaver/semiquaver figures as down, down up to achieve a more highly articulated interpretation. The cross-beat slurrings between bars 44 and 55 and in 81–86 are eminently practical and need no modification.

*Air*. This legato melody may be played as it comes nearly throughout, though bows may be retaken in bars 3, 8, 15 and 18.

*Gavotte I*. This again may be taken as it comes, preferably starting on the upbow. Two upbows will be needed in bar 9 and perhaps a downbow retake in bar 17.

*Gavotte II*. This is also playable as it comes, with retakes only in, say, bars 2, 7, 9, 18, 20 and 24.

*Bourrée*. If adjustments are made in bars 3, 11, 20, 23 and possibly 30, the movement again plays itself.

*Gigue*. Successive downbows need only be taken in bars 2, 21, 26, 32, 42, 44, 50 and 70.

Bow direction markings in baroque string music are exceptional, and are wholly absent in the music of Handel and Bach.


## ANALYSIS

There is of course a world of difference between a routine performance and an inspired interpretation. This is where analysis has an important function; there is a great deal to discover in each of the six movements. Bach's handling of phrase length, cadence, melodic line, key and texture all deserve the closest investigation (see above, p. 18 for a more extended discussion of analytical methods). There is, for instance, the way in which the key of D major is established at the very beginning of the first movement by means of a symmetrical opening four-bar phrase, in which the two principal figures of the section are introduced. From the fifth bar onward the two figures move inexorably through related keys without any firm cadence points, until the section ends expectantly on a half close. There is the perhaps obvious, but nonetheless miraculous way in which Bach draws out the opening four-bar phrase of the first Gavotte as the movement progresses. There is the marvellously simple shape, so gracefully ornamented, that underpins the melody of the Air. These and a host of other features need consciously to be recognised (and of course innately felt) if the performance is truly to be an authentic one.


## STRING ENSEMBLES

As we have already seen (p. 25 above), the string ensembles that Lully and Corelli directed were renowned for the disciplined perfection of their playing. Lully established in the 1650s a select group of sixteen strings from the twenty-four players of the royal band – *les petits violons*, as they were called. Corelli, who settled in Rome during the 1680s, led a string band of some twenty-eight players at a public concert in 1692 – seventeen violins, four violas and five lower strings (perhaps four cellos and a violone). The ensemble of St Peter's, Bologna, where the concerto grosso was born and where Corelli spent four years at the beginning of his career, numbered between ten and fifteen strings. Much larger groups were to be heard in the major musical centres on special occasions. No fewer than forty-five strings played at an important service at Bologna in 1708, for instance. A group of similar size was involved in a performance at Rome in the same year as Handel's *La Resurrezione*. At a private concert given by the Queen of Sweden, Corelli's concerti grossi were played by no fewer than 150 strings![3]

In England, too, string groups fluctuated in size, though none could match the 1708 orchestra at Rome. Charles II started off by emulating Louis XIV's *Vingtquatre violons*, though his aspirations rapidly proved to be bigger than his purse! To judge from the admittedly somewhat sparse evidence that has survived, Handel's average string group seems to have numbered between twenty and thirty players, upper strings predominating. However, the *Deborah* orchestra of 1733 shows that Handel had no objection to larger forces when these were available! (See the discussion of *Messiah* below, p. 90.)

Bach, on the other hand, never seems to have been able to command anything but the most modest forces. The Weimar strings probably numbered no more than a dozen. The Köthen establishment comprised two solo violins ('Kammermusiker') and four ripienists ('musici'). At Leipzig Bach became so frustrated with the instrumental forces that were available to him that he presented a report to the town councillors setting out his specific requirements and stating in what ways the current provisions fell short. Although in his report he envisaged no more than six upper strings, it is difficult to believe that he would have objected to further players had they been available. He well knew what was going on in Dresden, and he probably had as his ideal the court orchestra there, which at the time that he presented his B minor Kyrie, Gloria and Credo to the new Elector of Saxony, comprised a string group of more than twenty players.[4]

Broadly speaking, string groups tended to be relatively small in size and slightly top-heavy by modern standards. Sufficient exceptions can be found in Table 3, however, to warn against any attempt to dogmatise. Evidently the Italians did enjoy a gargantuan festival once in a while. Handel perhaps caught a taste for the colossal from Italy when he staged the 1733 performances of *Deborah*. Clearly music, like politics, was very much an art of the possible. Bach's ensemble was smaller by far than any of the other important European ensembles. Was this a matter of necessity, or did Bach really consider small to be beautiful? Certainly, the existence of only single parts to the orchestral suites and Brandenburg concertos suggests that early performances of these pieces were probably given by soloists – or at the most with two players to a part. As Bach had nothing against augmenting the Prelude of the E major Partita for solo violin into a concerto for organ, strings, woodwind and trumpets, would he have been likely to cavil at a modest increase in the size of the string group for the concertos and suites?

However, when the performing group was a small one, as it often was, the balance between strings and other instruments was undoubtedly very different to that heard in modern symphony orchestra performances of baroque music. Oboes and bassoons would have added a much more tangible reediness to the total ensemble (see below, p. 151 for a discussion of wind and brass instruments); and though trumpets would certainly have added excitement to the total sound, they would not have had quite that dominating brilliance that is often cultivated by modern players. What is often forgotten is that Bach saw nothing odd in blending recorder, oboe, violin and trumpet as equal solo instruments in the Second Brandenburg Concerto.

Table 3. Some string groups, *c.* 1650–1750

| | | | |
|---|---|---|---|
| 1656 | Paris | court | 16–21 ('Les petits violins du Roi' – Lully) |
| 1657 | Bologna | church | 6–11: 2–5 vns, 2–4 vas, cello, violone (the cathedral ensemble of San Petronio – Torelli, Corelli) |
| 1662 | London | court | 24 (the 24 Violins – Locke) |
| 1670 | London | Chapel Royal | 6: 5 'violins' and a violone (Locke, Blow, Purcell) |
| 1692 | Rome | concert | 28: 17 vns, 4 vas, 7 lower strings (directed by Corelli) |
| 1708 | Bologna | church | 42: 24 vns, 6 vas, 6 cellos, 6 violones (the cathedral ensemble of San Petronio – Torelli, Albinoni) |
| 1714 | Paris | opera | 27: 12 vns, 7 vas, 8 cellos and basses (Lully) |
| 1715 | Weimar | court | c. 10 (Bach) |
| 1720 | Köthen | court | 6: 2 solo vns, 4 ripienists (Bach) |
| 1728 | London | opera | 29: 22 vns, 2 vas, 3 cellos, 2 violones (Handel) |
| 1730 | Leipzig | church | 11–13: 2–3 vn1, 2–3 vn2, 2 va1, 2va2, 2 cellos, bass (Bach) |
| 1733 | London | opera | 40 (Handel's *Deborah*) |
| 1734 | Dresden | court | 23: 12 vns, 4 vas, 5 cellos, 2 violones (Vivaldi, Hasse, Pisendal) |
| 1751 | Paris | opera | 34: 16 vns, 6 vas, 7 cellos, 5 basses (Rameau) |
| 1754 | London | concert | 24: 14 vns, 5 vas, 3 cellos, 2 basses (*Messiah*, conducted by Handel) |
| 1770 | Winchester | cathedral | 39: 32 upper strings, 5 cellos, 2 basses (performance of Handel's *Joshua*) |

# 6

## Handel's *Messiah*

So far there has been no occasion to say anything about two important matters that will need investigation in this chapter: choral ensembles and voice production.[1] The choirs for Handel's oratorios were invariably drawn from cathedrals and chapels. This meant that boys always sang the treble [soprano] parts and adult males the alto parts. As we shall see, though, Handel sometimes required his soloists to sing with the choir. Surprisingly little is known of the choirs that took part in Handel's oratorios.[2] The first *Messiah* performance took place in Dublin, the chorus being recruited from the two cathedral choirs of Christ Church and St Patrick's. Assuming that all the Gentlemen took part, the chorus would have numbered about twenty-four men and ten choristers. The London performance of 1754 at the Foundling Hospital, on the other hand, for which unusually complete accounts have survived, involved a comparatively small chorus of six Chapel Royal boys and thirteen men. These sang against an orchestra of fifteen violins, five violas, three cellos, two double basses, four bassoons, four oboes, trumpets and drums; it is hardly surprising, then, that the five soloists – Signoras Frasi, Passerini (sopranos) and Galli (contralto), John Beard (tenor) and Robert Wass (bass) also 'assisted' in the choruses.

Since Handel was often happy to entrust the tenor and bass solos to gentlemen of the participating choirs, we may assume that the best cathedral singers were no mere amateurs. Just how they were trained, or who trained them, is unknown, however. Italian methods of voice production and ornamentation had certainly been familiar to the Gentlemen of the Chapel Royal since the 1630s, and it is clear from Henry Playford's *Brief Introduction to the Skill of Musick* (1664) that the tradition was still alive after the Restoration.

There were several seventeenth-century music instruction books in English that dealt briefly with singing. Their advice, however, was invariably to do with the pitching of intervals and such rudiments of music as were necessary for good sight singing. As far as voice production was concerned, Humphrey Bathe's *A Brief Introduction to the Skill of Song* (1597) said more than most:[3]

1. Practise to sunder the vowels and consonants, distinctly pronouncing them according to the manner of the place.
2. Practise to have the breath long to continue, and the tongue at liberty to run.
3. Practise at striking [i.e. keeping time] to keep a just proportion of one stroke to another.
4. Practise to have your voice clear.

What an English choir sounded like, therefore, is anybody's guess. Some hints are perhaps to be found in the balance between men and boys that was considered acceptable. In most choirs, including the *ad hoc* 1754 choir at the Foundling Hospital performance of *Messiah*, the ratio of men to boys was just over 2:1, although in a few cases, such as the Chapel Royal and the two Dublin choirs, it was almost as high as 3:1. Present-day ratios are very different. At best, in such choirs as King's and St John's Colleges, Cambridge, the ratio is about 1:1; in many choirs, however, it is 1:2 or more. Clearly, seventeenth- and eighteenth-century choirmen must have sung in a comparatively restrained manner, if the boys were not to be swamped. It could be, of course, that choristers then sang more aggressively. If that had been so, however, their tone would hardly have been described as 'sweet', a term which recurs again and again in contemporary commentaries.

The first book in English to deal in any detailed way with voice production was Pier Francesco Tosi's *Observations on the Florid Song . . . useful for all Performers, Instrumental as well as Vocal* (London, 1743),[4] a translation of the original *Opinioni de cantori antichi e moderni* (Bologna, 1723). The Italian composer, singer and teacher Tosi (1646–1732) settled in London in 1693, where he remained almost to the time of his death in 1732. He therefore saw Handel's early successes in England, and he must have trained a good many London singers, if no others. His singing method relates closely to styles of Italian singing that would have been known to Handel, and doubtless to Bach as well. The German musician Johann Galliard, who settled in London at about the same time as Tosi and who was closely associated with Handel's music, was responsible for the English translation. Tosi's work was widely read, and indeed it was still highly enough regarded in 1757 for Bach's former pupil Johann Friedrich Agricola to publish a German version under the title of *Anleitung zur Singkunst*.

Tosi had very clear ideas about the faults that singers should avoid: awkward posture, ugly facial expressions, throaty and nasal sounds, bad diction and poor breath control. He believed that singing was a demanding occupation requiring 'so strict an application that one must study with the mind when one cannot study with the voice' (chap. 6, para. 11). His aim was to develop vocal range, dynamic control and an ability to sustain long notes perfectly evenly. Range was to be extended by means of scales ('sol-fa', as they called it), the upper notes being sung with 'softness' to avoid 'screaming'. Dynamic control was to be achieved by practising the *Messa di Voce*, or, as Galliard and the English called it, 'the art to put forth the voice'. This involved singing a single note, starting with 'the softest *piano*', increasing to 'the loudest *forte*', and then decreasing to the original *piano*. Pitch steadiness was to be developed by holding single notes as long as possible on the three open vowels (a, o and u). Tosi identified three styles of voice production: the *di petto* manner, involving the 'full voice from the breast by strength'; the *di testa* manner, sound being produced 'more from the throat than the breast, and capable of more volubility' [i.e. agility]; and the *falsetto* manner, in which the 'feigned voice' is used, a voice that is formed entirely in the throat and has 'more volubility than any other but no substance' (chap. 1, para 18). Tosi observed that the 'full, natural' soprano voice stopped at C or D in the treble stave; the use of the 'feigned' falsetto voice was therefore essential to extend the range upward. A good teacher, he said, would aim 'so to unite the feigned and natural voice that they may not be distinguished', though how precisely this was to be done he did not, alas, explain![5]

Reading between the lines, we must suppose that Tosi cannot have been greatly interested in sheer volume of sound, or he would have given a good deal more attention than he did to breath control. Indeed, he almost completely ignored the existence of the lungs. To be sure, he recommended that singing should always be done standing up, and that breathing should be carefully worked out for each piece. Nowhere, though, did he describe the physical process of breathing.

Tosi placed good intonation at the top of his list of vocal skills (chap. 1, para. 13). This was to be achieved through singing scales, great care being taken to distinguish, as all good string players did, between the major semitone (5/9ths of a tone) and the minor semitone (4/9ths of a tone). In this respect, Tosi felt that the 4/7:3/7 proportion adopted by many of his contemporaries lacked subtlety. The two kinds of semitone are identified thus: 'the Semitone major changes name, line and space [e.g. D sharp to E]; the semitone minor changes neither' [e.g. F to F sharp]. Tosi's acidic comments on intonation suggest that by no means all singers achieved his exacting standards! (cf. wind intonation, p. 154).

Tosi said surprisingly little about diction, vital as this is in the shaping of the sound that the singer produces. Such comments as he made, indeed, are buried in the chapter on improvised ornament, his main concern being to pronounce double consonants: e.g. 'error', nor 'eror', and 'dally', not 'daly'.

Almost half of the book is devoted to ornamentation, an apt reminder of one very important but now unfamiliar role that the singer was then expected to play in performance. The composer was to provide the framework of the composition; it was, however, the singer's task to breathe life into it by means of embellishment.[6] Tosi began by discussing the two basic ornaments: the appoggiatura (chapter 2) and the trill (chap. 3). He then went on to explain in the fourth, seventh and eighth chapters how to improvise more extended passages in the Italian manner. At no point did he attempt to lay down strict procedures, nor are his few musical examples more than general indications of how the singer might realise an ornament, for, as he constantly repeated, such things are best learned by listening to expert singers and instrumentalists. He regarded the art of ornamentation, then, as a creative art. Slavishly to copy what others had done was to miss the point entirely. This is immediately evident from the very free way in which he approached the appoggiatura, which he considered was the most useful of all the ornaments. The word 'appoggiatura', he observed, comes from *appoggiare* (to lean on). The singer, therefore, was to lean on the first note, lingering rather longer on it than on the second – the note of resolution. Tosi's simple examples show that singers used both conjunct and disjunct appoggiaturas, perhaps even indulging in slight *portamenti* [i.e. slides] between the first and second notes.[7]

Tosi supplied examples of eight kinds of trill or shake (see Example 62). They further confirm what we have already discovered: that ornament was very much a matter of fashion, differing from country to country, and indeed from composer to composer and performer to performer. The first two examples represent Tosi's two principal trills – the Shake Major and the Shake Minor. Points to note about the eight kinds of trill include:

> (i) the equal possibility of beginning on the main note, or on the tone or semitone above the main note;
> (ii) the use of the major semitone (see above, p. 84) for semitone trills;
> (iii) the choice (depending on musical context) of long or short trills;
> (iv) the sharpening of the short trill by a rapid increase in speed;
> (v) the variation of the trill by mixing into it additional notes, as in Example 62, no. 8 – [a 'redoubled' trill]; and
> (vi) the addition of a turn at the end of the trill, termed a *trillo mordente* – this, he observed, was 'more taught by nature than art', the final notes being sung 'with more velocity than the others'.

Tosi also listed other trills that in his view were either old-fashioned or lacking in taste. There was the slow shake (Example 62, no. 7), which gradually accelerated; this, he argued, was little more than 'an affected waving', to be used only occasionally. There was also the rising and descending shake, in which the voice ascended and descended 'imperceptibly from

**Ex. 62**   Tosi's trills

Comma to Comma'. There was of course no precise way of notating this curious ornament; Example 62, Nos. 5 and 6 can only be an approximation of the effect.

Tosi devoted a lengthy chapter to Divisions, that is to say, improvisations upon simple melodic lines and figures (see above, p. 41 for further discussion of this point). He refused, however, to print any examples, on the grounds that even if a thousand of the most 'exquisite' passages of different sorts were written down, they would not serve for all purposes; moreover, 'there would always be wanting that spirit which accompanies extempore performances and is preferable to all servile imitations'. Handel's celebrated castrato, Guadagni, was famous for his improvised divisions, three examples of which were copied down by an admirer. One of these is given in Example 63.[8] No doubt Tosi had this kind of ornamentation in mind.

Tosi considered divisions to be decorative rather than expressive, their 'sole and entire beauty' springing from the fact that they were to be sung 'perfectly in tune, marked, equal, distinct and quick'. He nonetheless valued them highly, for when 'well executed in their proper place', they deserved

**Ex. 63** Improvised ornament in Handel's 'Alla fama'

applause and made the singer 'more universal; that is to say, capable to sing in any style'. He described two ways of singing divisions: in a 'marked' or a 'gliding' manner. The marked style was 'something like the *Staccato* on the Violin, but not too much'; the gliding style was like 'several notes in one stroke of the bow on the violin'. Glidings were similar in effect to string slurs. Intervals larger than a perfect fourth, however, were too great to be sung in a gliding style. Both styles of division were to be sung to 'a', 'e' or 'o' (prefer- ably 'a'), care being taken to avoid any initial aspirate or consonant such as 'ha, ha, ha' or 'gha, gha, gha'.

In the chapter on cadences (chap. 6; see also chap. 8) Tosi criticised the way in which so many singers over-ornamented their parts; the air to which he refers here is evidently in da capo (ABA) form.

> Every air has at least three cadences that are all three final [i.e. the cadences at the end of each of the three sections]. Generally speaking the study of the singers of the present times consists in terminating the *cadence* of the first part with an overflowing of *passages* and *divisions* at pleasure, and the *orchestra* waits; in that of the second the dose is increased, and the *orchestra* grows tired; but on the last *cadence* the throat is set going like a weathercock in a whirlwind, and the *orchestra* yawns. But why should the world be thus continually deafened with so many *divisions*?

Tosi deplored the fact that composers and singers so often failed to distinguish in their written and improvised figuration between the 'lively and various' theatre style, the 'delicate and finished' chamber style and the 'moving and grave' church style. He particularly recommended simple appoggiaturas and trills. He suggested, too, that ornamentation should be increased as the movement progressed: a few simple ornaments 'of good taste' in the first section; a few more 'artful' graces in the second; with extensive ornamentation in the da capo repeat. Indeed, a singer who failed to improve the original, he maintained, was 'no great master'. The utmost care was to be taken throughout to avoid 'injuring' the time, and when obbligato instruments were used, the styles of instrumental and vocal ornamentation should be carefully matched.

Although Bénigne de Bacilly's *Remarques curieuses sur l'art de bien chanter* (1668)[9] more properly belongs to the Paris of Lully's day, it may usefully serve as a supplement to Tosi, particularly in respect of diction, which the latter so badly neglects. Bacilly (*c.* 1625–90) settled in Paris shortly before 1650. His book is one of the very earliest singing tutors of any substance. Evidently it met a real need, for it was reprinted no fewer than three times before 1700. Bacilly assumes that singing is more a question of inborn talent than of hard work (chap. 8, p. 49), whereas Tosi speaks of the need for continuous study. Indirectly perhaps this is a further reflection on the reported difference between the 'dynamic' Italians and the 'lyrical' French.

The great strength of Bacilly's book is its extensive discussion of the way in which consonants and vowels may be used to colour a performance. Although of course Bacilly was writing about the pronunciation of French, much of his advice applies to any sung language, and it is just as important today as it has ever been. He dealt first with vowels. Bad teachers, he observed, constantly tell their pupils to 'open their mouths', unaware of the fact that different vowels need different degrees of openness, and indeed that one and the same vowel may call for different apertures, depending on its context. Take, for instance, the exclamation 'Ah!' in the following two passages:

'Ah! qu'il est malaise' (Ah! How uneasy he is) and
'Ah! qu'il est doux' (Ah! How gentle he is).

The first 'Ah' should be sung with a wide open mouth. This will give a hard edge to the sound, thereby underlining the sense of 'malaise'. The second should be sung with a mouth that is shaped to smile, so as to brighten the 'ah'. Each vowel must be correctly formed in the mouth; 'i' must be placed, for instance, at the front of the throat, care being taken to avoid a nasal quality; 'o' must be formed at the back of the throat, and so on (chap. 3). Vowel shapes are not to be changed while they are being sung [a common problem in English, where such words as 'fine' easily come to sound like 'fieeene']. Words in which two different vowel sounds follow in succession [diphthongs] are to be treated with the greatest care. The change from first to second vowel must not be dragged out: the two-syllable word 'vie', for instance, should be sung crisply, a sharp distinction being made between the 'i' and the 'e' by inserting a 'y' between them: thus, 'vi-ye'.

Bacilly was keenly aware of the expressive power of consonants, and especially of an effect that he called *gronger*, namely the emphasis and prolongation of a consonant, especially 'm' or 'n', before a vowel. The impact of 'mourir' (to die) could greatly be increased, for example, by sustaining the 'm' beyond its written length, and singing the vowel after it at the latest possible moment.

At the heart of Bacilly's concern for words lay an essential difference in national musical styles, for there is far less word repetition in French music than there is in other music of the period. In a sense, therefore, immediate intelligibility was far more important to the French than it was to other nationalities. Whether or not Tosi was consciously aware of this, he certainly paid far less attention to pronunciation than did Bacilly. Both Tosi and Bacilly were agreed, nonetheless, that the singer's main task was to get the *spirit* of the words across to the listener. The singer, like the orator, had to move and thus persuade the audience; simple audibility was by no means sufficient.

### THE TEXTUAL PROBLEM

Since Handel was more dependent on commercial success for his livelihood than were most of his contemporaries, it is perhaps understandable that he so frequently modified his oratorios and operas from performance to performance. Soloists were changed and movements were rewritten, added and deleted.[10] The final aria in *Messiah*, for instance – 'If God be for us' – was sung by 'The Boy' in the 1749 London performance; in 1752 it was sung by the operatic soprano, Signora Frasi, who also sang in a number of Handel's other oratorios; in 1753 it was sung by the castrato Guadagni. Handel was particularly impressed by Guadagni, rewriting and greatly extending the highly dramatic aria 'But who shall abide the day of his coming' for him. Guadagni was still at the time singing alto, though he later sang higher roles, and was the original Orfeo in Gluck's Italian version of the opera. Watkins Shaw's reconstructions of the *Messiah* casts from 1742–59[11] suggests that Italian sopranos probably took part in all but one of the performances, but that in the 1749 performance at least, a boy sang 'How beautiful are the feet' and 'If God be for us'. English sopranos were also heard at the first Dublin and London performances in 1742 and 1743, but not thereafter. Handel does not seem to have liked the English male alto sound either, for after the initial Dublin performances he engaged English and Italian contraltos and, in 1753 only, the castrato Guadagni. All his tenors and basses, however, seem to have been English.

In summarising the many options that are available, Shaw is against the idea of wholly free choice; on the other hand, he does not believe that Handel ever evolved a definitive version of the oratorio. It does seem, however, that after 1749 he discarded six movements: the aria setting of 'But lo, the angel of the Lord came upon them', the bass setting of 'But who may abide the day of his coming', the bass and soprano settings in D minor of 'Thou art gone up on high', and the 'stop-gap' recitatives 'But who may abide' and 'Thou shalt break them'. Moreover, it is unlikely that the *dal segno* aria for soprano, 'How beautiful are the feet' or the setting of 'O death where is thy sting' were ever used in performances directed by Handel. All these discarded movements may be found in the appendix to Shaw's *Textual Companion*. Shaw's full score of the *Messiah* (Novello, 1965) also contains alternative versions of movements that Handel is known to have used: 'Rejoice greatly', 'Thou art gone up on high', 'How beautiful are the feet' [two versions] and 'Their sound is gone out'.

*Messiah* is unique amongst Handel's oratorios in that an almost complete set of orchestral parts survives, as well as an autograph score and a conducting score in the hand of his amanuensis, J. C. Smith.[12] Although the parts were apparently never used, they were prepared for the Foundling Hospital under the terms of Handel's will (4 August 1757) and were probably copied from existing parts that had already been used for earlier Foundling Hospital performances. Many Bach autograph cantata scores are complemented by sets of parts that are either autograph or that carry corrections in Bach's hand. These Handel parts have not the same authority, for there is no reason to suppose that Handel could ever have checked them (he was practically blind by 1757). While they cannot be given priority over the autograph score or Handel's conducting score (copied directly from the autograph), they do convey important information that is wholly absent from the scores: namely that oboes and bassoons were used to support the strings and voices. For example, both scores of the chorus 'And the Glory of the Lord' (Shaw, no. 4) designate the three upper instrumental lines 'V1, V2, Viol', whilst the instrumental bass is unmarked. The Foundling Hospital parts, however, allot two bassoons to the bass line, and an oboe each to the first and second violins. The vocal parts are simply headed 'C, A, T, B'; two additional oboe parts (Set B in the Shaw edition) double the boys throughout. The oboes are used only in the Overture and choruses. The bassoons form part of the continuo and are used extensively throughout the oratorio. The wind parts well repay study, for they show how wind instruments might have been used in Handel's other oratorios. There is something to learn from the string parts, too: the *violino primo* and *secondo conc[er]tino* [1 each], *violino primo* and *secondo* [i.e. ripieno: two each], viola [two] and violoncello [two]. These confirm that Handel's careful markings of 'senza ripieno', and 'con ripieno per tutto' were indeed observed in performance, and that the distinction between tutti strings and a small concertino group should be scrupulously respected. As we know that Handel's 1754 orchestra comprised fifteen violins, five violas, three cellos and two double basses, the inference is that each of the string parts would have been shared by two players, the concertino comprising either the first desk or the leader of each department.

In most respects Handel's scores are accurate, explicit and easy to read. They do, however, present the reader with two specific problems: these concern slurring and overdotting. Handel added slurs very unsystematically to his scores. In many movements the inconsistencies cause no problems, for the unmarked figures have simply to be compared with similar earlier ones that are marked. 'But who may abide the day of his coming' is a case in point (Shaw, No. 6). Bars 77–90 of the original soprano version in G minor are fully slurred; in the identical bars of the D minor transposition for Guadagni (which Handel inserted into the J. C. Smith conducting score) slurs are applied only to the first quaver arpeggio of bar 77 and to the figures in bars 82 and 83. Had there been no G minor version, the solution to the D minor passage would have been obvious enough. The problem in many movements, however, is to decide whether inconsistencies are accidental or intentional. In the eighth bar of 'All they that see him' (Example 64), for instance, Handel has written an unslurred viola part, and in the ninth bar he

**Ex. 64**   Slurrings in Handel's 'All they that see him'

**Ex. 65**   Slurrings in Handel's 'Why do the nations'

has given no slurs at all. Smith, however, has slurred all the semiquavers of bars 8 and 9 in pairs.

A similar figuration occurs in bars 12 and 13 of 'Why do the nations' (Example 65). Did Handel deliberately leave out the slurs in the second bar of the first violin in order to underline the 'crescendo' effect of the figuration (Smith slurs both violin parts)? In the following movement – 'Let us break

**Ex. 66**    Articulation in Handel's 'Let us break their bonds asunder'

their bonds asunder' (Example 66) – did he place staccato dashes against the striding arpeggio figures of the first bar simply to reinforce the 'Allegro e staccato' instruction, or did he wish the concertino group to play the figure in an even more detached and emphatic way than the ripieno (from bar 3 onwards)?

In 'Every valley shall be exalted', should the paired quavers in the fourth and fifth bars be slurred simply because they are in bars 26–9? And how should the sixth and eighth bars be treated? Handel's own score is a bar longer at each point: J. C. Smith copied Handel's version into the conducting score, but then he pasted a blank piece of paper over the additional bars, presumably on Handel's instructions. Although Smith normally copied Handel's slurrings exactly, his slurrings differ here from Handel's. Are they to be regarded, like the pastings over, as Handel's own second thoughts? A different and very common problem is illustrated in the tenth bar of 'The people that walked in darkness', where the slurs are so hastily drawn that it is impossible to tell whether they cover the first three notes of the four-quaver groups or only the second and third. Handel's scores are full of such problems as these. It is vital, therefore, that the modern edition clearly defines (as Shaw does) the nature of the problems, for only then will the performer be in a position to make informed decisions.

### BOWING AND OVERDOTTING

Between 1706 and 1710 Handel spent some time in Italy, where he would have had many opportunities to experience the professionalism of Italian orchestral playing. There is every reason to suppose that he subsequently exacted similar standards from his English players. He would surely, then, have regarded bowing as an important ingredient of orchestral discipline, bowing based upon principles familiar to Lully and Corelli (see p. 26 above). As is the case with the music of these earlier composers, the only decisions that the modern string player has to take concern slurring consistency (discussed above) and bow direction – precisely where to retake an upbow or a downbow to ensure that downbows coincide with important downbeats (only in exceptional circumstances should clearly marked slurring be modified). A few typical movements may serve by way of example, taken from the first violin part [the bar number and beat are given, in that order]:

Overture
    retake downbows in 2:2, 9:4, 45:2, 46:2, 70:4, 87:2, 96:2
    retake upbows in 21:4, 25:4, 54:4, 81:4
    begin an upbeat on a downbow in 32:2, 34:2, 36:2, 48:2, 75:2, 79:2

'Comfort ye':
    retake upbows in bars 3 and 29 (demisemiquaver and semiquaver), 11:3
    retake downbows in bars 5:1, 7:3, 14:1

'Ev'ry valley':
    retake upbows in 34:2, 35:3, 65:2
    retake downbows in 14:1

'And the glory of the Lord':
    retake upbow in 38:2
    retake downbow in 40:2, 73:2

One further notational problem remains to be discussed: the controversial convention of overdotting. It is at its most acute in the French Overture, about which something has already been said (see above, p. 72). Would Handel's orchestra have played the opening Grave in the manner that Shaw suggests (he indicates this in small notation) or literally, according to Handel's notation (Example 67)? No complex discussions would have been needed in rehearsal to agree on the overdotting of the crotchet/quaver figures. But would the viola instinctively have known in bar 11 that the two quavers were to be played as a dotted figure? Two pairs of dotted quaver/

**Ex. 67**   Double dotting in the Overture of *Messiah*

semiquaver rhythms, after all, are fully written out in bar 8. And if the
quavers in bar 11 are to be played as written, what about the dotted
crotchet/quaver rhythms in the other parts? Perhaps there was no *one* way of
playing French overtures? Avison, after all, argued that composers and
players should carefully distinguish between the chamber, the operatic and
the church styles. Was Handel's unusual 'Grave' a warning to players that
the music was to be taken at an appropriately 'devotional' speed – and even
perhaps that the notation was to be interpreted literally?

There are many other places in *Messiah* where the rhythmic implications
of the notation are not entirely clear. 'The Lord gave the word', for instance,
is often sung in overdotted rhythms, as in Example 68.

**Ex. 68**   Double dotting in 'The Lord gave the word'

Certainly this is a *possible* solution, though it is one that may well have been more common during the second half of the century than during Handel's lifetime (see p. 72 above).

As we have already seen, there is plenty of evidence to show that passages of undotted rhythms were frequently 'jazzed up' in performance (see above, p. 66). Variants in the two published versions of Handel's Op. 1 No. 1 Sonata (Example 69) show how this might have been done.

**Ex. 69**   Dotting in two versions of Handel's Sonata Op. 1: Larghetto

Might then the strings have dotted the upbeat figures in bars 5, 6, 8 and 9 of 'I know that my redeemer liveth' (Example 70)? In this case the answer is probably no, since Handel continues throughout the movement to use both the dotted and the undotted versions of these figures, as if deliberately seeking to avoid regularising the rhythm.

**Ex. 70**  Dotting in Handel's 'I know that my redeemer liveth'

Oddly enough, rests are never dotted in eighteenth-century notation. In such a context as 'Behold the Lamb of God' (Example 71, cf. also 'Surely he hath borne our griefs' and 'The trumpet shall sound') the opening of the first violin part may possibly have been understood as a double dotted crotchet rest followed by semiquaver G:

**Ex. 71**  Dotting in Handel's 'Behold the Lamb of God'

There is a danger, however, of turning this supposed convention into a rule. Take, for instance, the opening of the autograph version of 'Thus saith the Lord' (Example 72). If Handel knew that his players would automatically play the opening as dotted quaver/semiquaver, why did he bother to write this rhythm out in full in the third bar? And, although in theory at least there is nothing wrong with the editorially double dotted rhythms of 'Lift up your heads' shown in Example 73, would the words really have been snatched in that way? Perhaps then, 'improvised overdotting' should be practised with great restraint, individual taste being the final arbiter?

**Ex. 72**   Dotting in Handel's 'Thus saith the Lord'

**Ex. 73**   Dotting in Handel's 'Lift up your heads'

CONTINUO

A word is needed at this point about figured bass accompaniment, since keyboard continuo supplies the foundation to almost all music of the high baroque. Bach's violin, gamba and flute sonatas (BWV 1014–20, 1027–9 and 1030–2) are practically the only compositions of the period in which the keyboard part is fully written out. Most continuo parts take the form of a bass line with figures underneath the notes to indicate what harmonies are to be played. Most modern editors realise these figured basses into keyboard notation, since few players now have the skill to improvise their parts above the basses. Printed realisations vary greatly in quality. Some, like Telemann's, which he published specifically as models for his contemporaries to copy, are exceedingly ponderous and show no awareness of the importance of vertical density as accent (on such an instrument as the harpsichord, accentuation is achieved partly by thickening the vertical textures, whilst upbeats are best realised in simple two- and three-part textures). Other realisations, like the ingenious Purcell Society continuo to the *Fairy Queen* shown in Example 74 (Act. 2, sc. 1: 'Come all ye songsters'), do not lie easily under the hands, and could never have been improvised on the spot.

**Ex. 74**    Continuo realisation in Purcell's 'Come all ye songsters'

In the case of the Purcell, the editors obviously did not heed C. P. E. Bach's warning against fancy realisation:

> Gratuitous passagework and busy noise do not make a beautiful accompaniment. In fact they harm the principal part by robbing it of its freedom to introduce variations and repetitions. The accompanist will achieve distinction . . . by letting intelligent listeners hear an unadorned steadiness and noble simplicity in a flowing accompaniment, an accompaniment that does not interfere with the brilliance of the principal part. He will not be forgotten. No! A perceptive listener will not readily miss anything, melody and harmony being for him inseparable. [*Versuch*, chap. 4, p. 367]

Several early eighteenth-century musicians published valuable comments on style in continuo playing.[13] Broadly speaking, style in figured bass playing depends on half a dozen general precepts: (i) the accompaniment should *accompany* and not compete with the solo lines; (ii) the right hand should therefore normally lie below the upper solo line or (if the solo voices and instruments are in the tenor and bass registers) keep within the octave above them; (iii) the right hand should not normally double a solo line;

(iv) only when the soloists are resting should any elaborate realisation be attempted, developing, if possible, figures that have already been heard; (v) harpsichord realisations should complement the phrasing of the solo lines, particularly by varying the density of keyboard textures, and (vi) organ realisations should not normally exceed four-part chords, and registrations for solo instruments and voices should be restricted to 8' and 8'+4' registers.

Johann Philipp Kirnberger's version of the continuo part of Bach's *Musical Offering* will repay some study, for it has the quality of an honest if somewhat pedestrian realisation (see Example 75). The chords fit easily under the right hand, with the left hand playing a single line for most of the time. Most importantly, the realisation mirrors the harmonic rhythm of the

**Ex. 75**    Kirnberger's realisation of the continuo of Bach's *Musical Offering* BWV 1079a

opening, in which harmonic movement takes place on the first and second beats of the bar rather than the first and third. Moreover, Kirnberger places the thickest chords on accented beats, whilst generally keeping the right hand below the upper solo line.

As recitative is normally the vehicle for the unravelling of plot, and as recitative words are rarely repeated, recitative accompaniment must be unobtrusive in order to secure maximum audibility. Eighteenth-century players often did no more than play short, simple chords to mark each chord change, even though the figured basses might be notated in semibreves and minims. In his *Neu erfundene und gründliche Anweisung* of 1711 Johann David Heinichen recommended that chords should be lifted as soon as they are played, rests taking the place of notes so that the singer may be the better heard. When the continuo keyboard was organ, short punctuating chords could also serve to alleviate the otherwise 'monotonous hum' of the pipes. Both Friedrich Erhard Niedt (1721) and Mattheson (1739) confirm the practice of chord shortening, which was still being recommended by Türk as late as 1787.

Attention should be paid, incidentally, to the way Handel notated recitative cadences (a matter on which, exceptionally, the Shaw edition is unhelpful). In places, he obviously wanted the V/I progression to synchronise with the voice and not to wait for it to finish. The recitative 'And the angel said unto them' is a typical case in point (Example 76).

**Ex. 76**  Recitative cadences: Handel's 'And the angel said unto them'

While Niedt and Mattheson both accepted the harpsichord as an appropriate continuo instrument in church, Bach normally used the organ.[14] In the theatre and concert hall (where Handel's oratorios were often performed), the harpsichord and cello were the principal continuo instruments. Although the gentlemen of the Dublin cathedrals formed the chorus at the first performance of *Messiah*, the event took place in the new music rooms at Fishamble Street. All the early London performances, too, took place either at Covent Garden or at the King's Theatre. In all probability, both harpsichord and organ were used – organ for the choruses and harpsichord for the solo movements and recitatives.

# 7

## Bach's C minor Passacaglia BWV 582

Just as there were distinctively national styles of performance, so in many cases were there distinctively national styles of musical instrument. Certainly French organs had their own clearly defined characteristics, and these differed markedly from those of Italian organs. Certainly, too, French and Italian influences are observable in German organ design, just as they are observable in German music. German organs were no mere syntheses of other national types, however. As we shall see, their very variety presents the Bach interpreter with major problems. The great instruments of Bach's elder contemporary Arp Schnitger are uniquely North German and were unrivalled in the comprehensiveness of their pedal departments. Bach had many opportunities to admire Schnitger's work at Lüneburg, Lübeck and Hamburg. After he settled in Leipzig in 1723 he came to know the work of his equally famous central German contemporary Gottfried Silbermann, whose instruments speak with a markedly French accent. Both the German and the French traditions need to be understood in relation to Bach's music.[1]

The history of the organ is the history not only of its builders, its players and its composers, but also of its liturgical function. During the early eighteenth century, for instance, the principal role of the English cathedral organ was to accompany the choir (and to a lesser extent the congregation) in the daily choral services. For this reason the organ was therefore sited on a screen (or wall) close to the singers. It had only a secondary role as a solo instrument; it therefore remained comparatively small in size until the development of 'symphonic' accompaniments in the nineteenth century. Few English organs even had pedals before 1800. In Lutheran worship, on the other hand, there was plenty of scope for solo organ music. By 1700, therefore, German organist-composers had developed techniques of organ composition and performance that were highly idiomatic – notably in the use of pedals. Many German Lutheran churches housed large organs of sixty stops or more, particularly those in the wealthy North German Hansa ports. A large organ, after all, was both an oral and an aural witness to the business acumen, piety and artistic sensibility of the community!

## The French organ, c. 1650–1750, and Gottfried Silbermann

The French tradition is comparatively easy to discuss, for French builders followed a standardised design, and French composers generally specified the stops (i.e. the tone colours) that were to be used at any given time. The remarkably colourful character of the French organ is well illustrated by the specification of the instrument at St Louis des Invalides, Paris (1679–87), described by Peter Williams as an 'accomplished' example of the French classical organ. It had three manuals and pedals, each manual having a particularly well developed array of flute stops.

Organ at St Louis des Invalides, Paris (1679–87)

Grand Orgue (Compass CD–c''')
Principal chorus: montre 16, montre 8, prestant 4, doublette 2, fourniture (4 ranks) and cymbale (3 ranks)
Flutes: bourdon 16, bourdon 8, flute 4, grosse tierce, nazard, quarte de nazard 2, tierce, cornet (5 ranks)
Reeds: trompette 8, clairon 4, voix humaine 8

Echo (c–c''')
cymbale (2 ranks)
bourdon 8, flute 4, nazard, quarte 2, tierce.
cromorne 8

Positif (CD–c''')
montre 8, prestant 4, doublette 2, fourniture (3 ranks), cymbale (2 ranks)
bourdon 8, flute 4, nazard, tierce, larigot.
cromorne 8, voix humaine 8

Recit (c'–c''')
cornet (5 ranks), trompette 8

Pedale (AA–f' – 30 notes)
Flute 8, trompette 8.

Such an organ as this offers a particularly wide range of melodic colours; it is richly endowed with mutations (flute stops pitched at a fifth or major third from the fundamental) and reeds. Its very small pedal department is primarily melodic (for the performance of plainsong cantus firmi), and its tutti manual sonorities are better suited to broadly moving harmonies than to intricate contrapuntal textures. Its mixtures (both the *fourniture* and the *cymbale*) are low pitched in their upper registers in comparison with those of German organs of the period, and they add fullness rather than brilliance.

Suggested registrations of individual pieces are to be found in practically every French book of organ music published between 1660 and 1760. In certain cases, composers felt strongly enough about the sounds that they wanted to warn players against tackling pieces unless all the necessary stops were available to them.[2] Others, such as André Raison, took a more relaxed view of registration, and were quite happy for pieces to be played on manuals other than those specified, provided that due care was taken to play the music in an appropriate style.[3]

Fenner Douglas helpfully groups French registrations into four texture-based categories: broad [full, largely chordal] textures, contrapuntal textures, melodic textures and composite textures. In the first category come registrations described as *plein jeu*, *grand jeu* and *fond d'orgue*. The fullest of these was *grand jeu*, dominated by the *grand orgue trompettes*, supported variously by flue stops, including in certain cases the *cornet*, to fill out the rather weak trebles of the reeds. *Plein jeu* invariably meant full principal chorus, upwards from 16' pitch on both *grand orgue* and *positif* (coupled, without reeds), against which the pedal 8' reed could stand in cantus firmus pieces. Slowly moving, richly harmonic pieces were played on *plein jeu*, which apparently was never used for fugues or other kinds of music. Fugues were registered on reeds, some supporting foundation stops probably being simultaneously drawn. The *fond d'orgue* comprised all the principals and flutes at 16', 8' and 4' pitches, the *positif* possibly being coupled to the *grand orgue*.

Registrations of the other three categories tend to be more exactly specified. *Cornets* and *tierces* were the most favoured timbres for melodic lines (*recits*): the *tierce* sounded two octaves and a third above 8' pitch, giving an unmistakably nasal quality to the sound. The *cornet* was a stop consisting of five separate flute ranks at 8', 4', 2⅔', 2' and 1⅗' pitches, placed on the *récit*. Most French organs of the period were so designed that individual stops could be drawn to make up a *cornet séparé* on at least one manual; this was possible, for instance, on both the *grand orgue* and *écho* manuals of the St Louis des Invalides organ mentioned above (a *cornet séparé* could also be simulated on the *positif*, though the 2' stop was a principal, not a flute). These composite *cornets* were less prominent than the single stop *cornet*, which normally had a limited compass of c'–c''', and which was mounted on a separate chest, so as to speak out boldly from the case. The *tierce* also featured in many other combinations of stops, ranging from a basic group of four stops (8', 4', 2⅔' and 1⅗') to as many as thirteen. A favourite sonority that drew from French composers some of their most poignant organ music was the 'Récit de tierce en taille': the *tierce* solo was placed in the tenor register, accompanied by quiet flute stops on pedals and right hand manual. The *nazard*, speaking at an octave and a fifth above the unison, was an equally colourful solo stop when combined with various flue stops of 8' and 4' pitch. Soft reeds, such as the *voix humaine* and *cromorne*, were also used as solo stops.

The specification of the organ at the Dresden Sophienkirche shows how greatly Silbermann was indebted to the French tradition. It was probably on this organ that Bach played to the Dresden court in 1725.[4]

*Gottfried Silbermann's organ at the Dresden Sophienkirche (1725)*

*Hauptwerk*
Principals: 8, 4, 2⅔, 2, Cimbel
Flutes: 16, 8 (two), 4, Terz, Cornet
Trompete: 8

*Oberwerk*
Principals: 8, 4, 2, Quint Mixtur
Flutes: 16, 8 (two), 4, Nasat
Vox humana, Unda Maris

*Pedal*
Principal 16, Sub-bass 16, Posaune 16, Trompete 8

together with manual to pedal couplers, and ventil mechanisms controlling the addition and subtraction of a limited number of stops.

## THE ORGAN IN SAXONY AND NORTH GERMANY

The pipes of the French organ were all placed within a single case. In North German and Dutch organs, however, a separate case was provided for the pipes of each manual. As Peter Williams points out in his *New History* (p. 99), one of the advantages of this so-called *Werkprinzip* design was that an organ could easily be enlarged. For this reason, perhaps, North German organs tended to be far less standardised than French ones. Probably for the same reason, German composers left the choice of stops to the player, knowing that each instrument would be different. Some idea of the problem can be got from a study of the organs that Bach himself played at Arnstadt, Mühlhausen, Weimar and Leipzig.

Oddly enough, not one of the instruments that Bach regularly played was in any way outstanding. To be sure, there were fine instruments at Lüneburg, where Bach was for three years a chorister, and at Hamburg, the great city-port that he visited several times from there, and where in 1720 he played before the 97-year-old Reinken. Bach must also have admired, and perhaps played, Buxtehude's magnificent instrument in the Marienkirche at Lübeck, where he spent the Advent and Christmas of 1707. The disposition of this organ is given by Kerala J. Snyder.

*Buxtehude's organ at Marienkirche, Lübeck*

*[Haupt]Werk*
Principals: 16, 8, 4, Mixtur, Scharff
Flutes: 16, 8, 4, Nazard, Rauschpfeiffe (possibly a soft principal chorus mixture)
Reeds: 16, 8, 8

*Brustwerk*
Principals: [8], 4, 2, Mixtur, Cymbel
Flutes: 8, 4, 2, Larigot
Other ranks: Sesquialtera, Krummhorn 8, Regal 8

*Ruckpositiv*
Principals: 8, 4, Mixtur, Scharff
Flutes: 16, 8, 8, 8, 2
Other ranks: Sesquialtera
Reeds: Dulcian 16, Baarpfeife 8, Regal 8, Vox humana 8

*Pedal*
Principals: 32, 16, 16, 8, 4, Mixtur
Flutes: 16, 8, 2
Reeds: 24, 16, 16, 8, 8, 2.[5]

Famed though Bach was as an organs advisor and recitalist, very little is known of his ideas on organ design. Perhaps his report on the Mühlhausen organ is the nearest we shall ever get to an understanding of the ideal Bach organ. Although Bach was organist there for barely a year, he did recommend various changes in the specification (marked * below). In its revised form, the comprehensive 3-manual instrument would have been extremely colourful, though it would have done no better than Silbermann's Sophienkirche organ (see above, p. 105) in soft trio combinations or in French music.

*Bach's organ at St Blasius, Mühlhausen*

*Hauptwerk*
Principals: 8, 4, *Nasat (to replace narrower Quint), 2, Mixtur, Zimbel, Sesquialtera
Flutes: 16, (8?) 4
*Gamba 8 (to replace Gemshorn)
*Fagott 16 (to replace 8 Trompete)

*Brustwerk*
Principals: 2, Mixtur
Flutes: 8, 4, Terz, Quint
Schalmei 8

*Ruckpositiv*
Principals: 4, 2, Zimbel
Flutes: 8, 8, 2, Quintflot
Salizional 4, Sesquialtera

*Pedal*
Principals: *32, 16, 8, 4, Mixtur
Flutes: 32, 16, 1
Reeds: 16, 8, 2

Most central and southern German organs were of comparatively modest

dimensions. Bach's Arnstadt instrument was the kind of organ that Pachel-
bel would have known: a two-manual instrument of 20–30 stops, with well
developed principal choruses on the manuals, little in the way of solo colour
(mutations and soft reeds) and a simple pedal of mainly 16' pitch.

### Bach's Arnstadt organ

*Hauptwerk*
Principals: 8, 4, Quint, Mixtur, Zimbel
Flutes: 8 (two?), 4
Viola da gamba, Gemshorn, Trumpet

*Brustwerk*
Principals: 4, 2, Mixtur
Flutes: 8, 4, 2, Quint (wider scale than the *Hptwk* Quint?)

*Pedal*
Principal: 8
Flutes: 16, 8
Violone, Posaune

The precise specifications of Bach's Leipzig instruments at the Thomas-
kirche and the Nikolaikirche are not known, though they are unlikely to have
been significantly more colourful or complete than that of the Arnstadt
instrument. None of the Leipzig area organs are likely to have had the
advantage of a *Rückpositiv* department, or of a well developed pedal organ.
Indeed, as Williams has pointed out, 'on no single organ that Bach is known
ever to have played would all of his music sounded at its best'.[6]

This is not the place to consider the technical intricacies of organ mechanisms. The crucial point to understand is that a finely built tracker mechanism of the kind that Schnitger and Gottfried Silbermann were building had a
sensitivity of touch that no later pneumatic or electrical substitute could
match. Precision of touch is as crucial to the organist as to the harpsichordist, for in both cases accentuation and articulation – and thus phrasing –
depend on the *exact* moment at which each note is attacked and released.

### SOURCES AND EDITIONS

A good deal has already been said about the need to procure reliable editions
that reflect as closely as possible the intentions of the composer (see above, p.
5). It is a sad fact that a large part of Bach's organ music has survived only
in secondary copies. The most interesting of these were, however, made by a
circle of pupils and friends, most of whom seem to have been fairly careful
copyists. This is the case for the BWV 582 Passacaglia, though the
Griepenkerl edition, published by Peters in 1844, claimed to be based on an
autograph owned by C. W. F. Guhr (since lost).[7] The earliest copy that

survives is that in the *Andreas Bach Book* [Leipzig, Musikbibliothek, MS III.8.4]. which is thought to date from about 1712. Two somewhat later copies were made by J. T. Krebs and J. F. Kittel, both of whom were pupils of Bach's. There are a further dozen late eighteenth-century copies. Close comparison of these sources reveals few variants of any substance, nor do they contain any substantial errors. Indeed the layout here and there suggests that the writer was attempting even to preserve the physical disposition of the original in his copy.

Typically, there are few articulation marks of any kind in any of these sources (see above, pp. 8 and 55 for discussions of keyboard articulation): all are slurrings, as listed below.

| | |
|---|---|
| bar 45, both hands | a pair of parallel semiquavers, in thirds, slurred together (Example 79) |
| bars 104–111, both hands | thirteen groups of four semiquavers, the second to fourth of each group being slurred (Example 78) |
| bar 169, left hand | the cross-beat slurring of the first two quavers in each of the four phrases of the countersubject (Example 77) |
| bar 255, right hand | the ornamental semiquaver/ demisemiquaver/semiquaver group on beat 2 |

Easily the most interesting of these is the cross-beat slurring of the first countersubject of the fugue (Example 77). This slurring is to be found in MS P320 – a late eighteenth-century copy possibly in the hand of Kittel, one of Bach's last pupils. It also appears in Griepenkerl's edition. Whether this effective, if eccentric phrasing was Kittel's, and whether Griepenkerl really did have access to a lost autograph we shall probably never know. Certainly if Bach had asked his pupils to phrase the countersubject across the beat, some indication of this would have been needed in the score, for it goes against the baroque practice of placing 'downbows' on the 'good' notes (see above, p. 26, for a discussion of the rule of the downbow and its implication

**Ex. 77**    Phrasing in a late eighteenth-century copy of Bach's Passacaglia BWV 582

**Ex. 78**    Phrasings in early eighteenth-century copies of the Passacaglia BWV 582

for norms of articulation). But what is the meaning of the other slurrings? Why that single pair in bar 45? (See Example 79.) Can it really be to distinguish it from all the other similar figures in that variation? And how

**Ex. 79**    Phrasings in early eighteenth-century copies of the Passacaglia BWV 582

exactly are the slurrings to be interpreted between bars 104 and 110 (Example 78)? C. P. E. Bach and Quantz refer to three levels of articulation (see above, p. 17). Is, then, the first semiquaver of each group (being unslurred) to be ever so slightly detached, in the manner of Quantz's 'normal' articulation? Is the first of the three slurred semiquavers to be held ever so slightly, in the way suggested by Quantz and Leopold Mozart? (see below, p. 126). Does the presence of these slurrings confirm that only in those places should the organist go for a true legato?

If no absolutely certain answers are possible to these questions, some clues are to be found here and there in the very textures that Bach employs. In bars 45, 49, 102–3, and 110–1 (shown in Examples 78 and 79), for instance, crossing parts imply the prerelease of certain notes. In parts of the thirteenth variation, and in bars 81 and 89, intervals that do not readily fall under the hand automatically produce articulations and phrasings.[8] Bach's own transcriptions for organ also provide a window into contemporary articulation practice.[9] Perhaps the most remarkable of these is the transformation of the Präludium of the E major Partita for Solo Violin BWV 1006 into the excitingly orchestrated Sinfonia to Cantata BWV 29. Here the organ takes over more or less note-for-note the solo violin part, reproducing exactly such bowings as there are in the original, with the exception of bars 105 to 130: the inclusion of these would presumably have obscured the clarity of the organ line. Other transcriptions, too, confirm the compatibility of string and keyboard articulations, notably the first movement of the E minor organ Trio Sonata BWV 528, which is also the Sinfonia to the second part of Cantata BWV 76, and the *Schübler* chorale preludes 'Wachet auf' and 'Meine Seele erhebt den Herrn', cantata bowing slurs being transferred to the organ transcriptions with only small variants.[10] Evidence of the kind, therefore, suggests that the organist would have respected the 'rule of the downbow' just as much as would the violinist. Bach's autograph parts for wind and stringed instruments, in other words, have much to teach the keyboard player.[11]

Apart from the countersubject slurring mentioned above, the most interesting variants concern ornamentation. Two of the dozen manuscripts (MSS P277 and P290) give a highly ornamented reading of the first fifty or so bars, one that suggests French influence.[12] Both sources, however, date from the second half of the century, and they may well reflect post-baroque tastes. The Mempell-Preller source of Bach's music, which dates from his lifetime, does, however, contain a fair amount of ornamentation.

### SONORITIES

Although German composers normally left the choice of registration to the performer (unlike their French contemporaries), certain aspects of registration were nonetheless governed by convention. Preludes and fugues were played boldly, using principal choruses and perhaps a pedal reed. Softer registrations of various kinds were available for trios and for solo music with accompaniment.[13] All the organs that Bach knew (indeed, all eighteenth century organs) were designed in such a way that the player could only with great difficulty change stops during a performance (see, for instance, the layout of Bach's Arnstadt console). The simplest way to alter registration was to change manual. French composers arranged their music so that this could easily be done. Manual changes are easy to manage, too, in Handel's organ concertos. In continuous, contrapuntal music, however, opportunities for change rarely occur, even in those large, concerto-like preludes and fugues of Bach's. In just one or two pieces a manual change is actually specified, but these exceptions seem to prove the rule, for in each case the layout of the music allows a comfortable (if speedy) change: Bach's 'Dorian' Toccata is a rare example of this.[14]

But how should a continuous variation form such as the C minor Passacaglia be registered? If there were breaks between the variations, as there are, for instance, in the magnificent 'Sei gegrüßt' variations, no one would possibly think of playing the entire piece on one *organo pleno* registration. But because of its continuous nature, Williams suggests the Passacaglia should be played throughout on one registration. There are, however, natural breaks in the music that allow for easy and musically convincing changes. Can it really have been the case that stop changes would *never* have been made, simply because they could not be controlled directly by the player? It would, after all, have been an unusual player who could have managed without a page turner, and the page turner could easily have done double duty as a stop puller. To be sure, most of Bach's organ compositions suggest a continuous, unaltered registration, but the Passacaglia *is* a variation form that offers many opportunities for change. There are of course many alternative ways of looking at the structure of the Passacaglia; five of these are shown below.

| interpreters | groupings |
| --- | --- |
| Geiringer | 1–5/6–10/11–15/16–20; with internal pairs 1–2/4–5/6–7/9–10/11–12/14–15/16–17/19–20 |
| Wolff | 1–2/3–5/6–9/10–11/12–15/16–18/19–20 |
| Vogelsänger | 1–2/3–5/6–8/9–12/13–15/16–18/19–20 |
| Klötz | 1–2/3–5/6–8/9/10–12/13–15/16–18/19–20 |
| Radulescu | 1–5/6–9/10–12/13–15/16–17/18–20 |

All five analyses (and there are other equally possible ones) are in their various ways 'right'. Each will govern the way in which the music is registered. Some players, like Williams, will see the Passacaglia as a continuum in which the prevailing dynamic is *forte*. Others will see variations 13–15 as a softer contrast to the outer variations. Others will seek to emphasise the Passacaglia's cumulative qualities, in which a steady crescendo is only interrupted temporarily in variations 13–15. At Mühlhausen, for instance, the following cumulative scheme would have been eminently practicable, leaving the organ assistant ample time to adjust stops and to turn pages:

[*B* = Brustwerk; *R* = Rückpositiv; *H* = Hauptwerk]

| Variation | registration |
|---|---|
| 0,1 | *B* 8 flute |
| 2 | *R* 8 flute |
| 3 | *H* 8 flute |
| 4 | *B* 8, 4 flutes |
| 5 | *R* 8, 4 flutes |
| 6 | *H* 8, 4 flutes |
| 7 | *R* 8+4 principals |
| 8 | *H* 8+4 principals |
| 9 | *R* 8+4 & 2 principals |
| 10 | *H* 8, 4, 2 principals (*RH*); *R* (LH as 9) |
| 11 | as 10, hands reversed |
| 12 | all on *H* |
| 13 | *R* 8, 4 flutes |
| 14–15 | *H* 8 flute; *B* 8 flute (both in variation 14; *B* only in variation 15) |
| 16–19 | *H* principals to mixture; adding Pedal 16 reed in 18; cymbal in 19 and Pedal 8 reed in 20 |

Whether or not such a scheme would have been adopted (and there is no way of proving or disproving it) there is no denying Bach's superb command of 'orchestral' colour. There is no denying either the fondness of his Italian contemporaries for dynamic nuances in orchestral music – and, especially, for tutti *crescendos* and *diminuendos* (see above, p. 38). It would be a bold critic, then, who maintained that registration changes were never used in the Passacaglia.

# 8

## Mozart's D minor String Quartet K421: a contemporary analysis

Charles Rosen's stimulating book *The Classical Style: Haydn, Mozart, Beethoven* (London, 1972) is compulsory reading for any performer with a serious interest in the so-called 'classical' period of music history. In no other are the distinctions between classical and baroque so clearly drawn:

> In most Baroque music [he writes], a relatively low level of tension is created and sustained, with certain fluctuations, only to be resolved at the end of the piece ... The emotional force of the classical style [however] is clearly bound up with the *contrast* between dramatic tension and stability.

The classical era of Haydn and Mozart was heralded by a preclassical period of experimentation in which many small but individual talents prospered. At the root of change was the new concept of musical expression that Rosen describes. Baroque composers such as Johann Mattheson had assumed that a self-contained movement would normally express only one mood (see the discussion of *Affekt*, pp. 18ff. above). By the 1750s, however, no such assumption could be made. Leopold Mozart, for instance, took it for granted that mood contrasts could be developed within a single movement:

> the greatest care must be taken [he wrote] to determine and communicate the *affects* which the composer wishes to portray; and as sadness often alternates with joy, every *affect* must be carefully depicted according to its character. In short, the player must play the piece in such a way that he is himself moved by it.[1]

But in what ways might a classical listener have been moved? To what extent would he have been aware of the musical processes that were at work in the music? Would our twentieth-century theories of classical form – and especially first-movement form, the most complex of all – have made sense to him? That people were deeply moved by great music is evident enough from the way in which such critics as C. F. Michaelis and E. T. A. Hoffmann wrote about it.[2] But in what sense were their flights of literary fancy grounded in a technical awareness of what was going on? One of the most

informative contemporary witnesses was the French theorist and critic
Jérome-Joseph de Momigny, whose sizeable *Cours complet d'harmonie et de composition* (Paris, 1806) deserves to be much better known than it is. Momigny,
who was six years younger than Mozart, began his career as organist of St
Pierre, Lyons. He settled in Paris in the 1790s and founded a publishing
house there in 1800.[3] His *Cours complet* contains a great deal of drily academic
instruction on harmony and counterpoint, to be sure, but it is at the same
time a remarkably perceptive work. Above all it contains extended analytical commentaries on the first movements of two outstanding classical compositions: Haydn's E flat 'Drum Roll' Symphony, and Mozart's D minor
Quartet K421, both of which illustrate how at least one informed eighteenth-
century musician approached the business of playing and listening to music.

Nowhere does Momigny use the terms exposition, development and
recapitulation that are familiar to us. Indeed, these somewhat misleading
terms are a post-classical invention, dating from a time when first movement
form was already passing into history. The terms are unsatisfactory, of
course, because they imply that the process of development was peculiar to
the second section of the movement, whereas a good deal of development
normally takes place in the first section, and even in the last – a fact that
Momigny fully appreciated! Not unsurprisingly perhaps, Momigny saw
first-movement form as a gigantic binary structure (this, after all, was its
origin), and he therefore termed the section before the double bar – i.e. the
exposition – the first *'reprise'* (viz. repetition), and the remainder the second
*'reprise'*, though by then the practice of performing even the exposition repeat
was by no means universal. He divided the second *reprise* into two (our
development and recapitulation) and he described the whole structure as an
edifice having a central dome (development) and two wings (exposition and
recapitulation).

Although Momigny was more concerned with phrase structure than with
key, he was certainly well aware of the tonal principles that underlay
first-movement form. As he observed in his analysis of the D minor Quartet:

> The whole of [the exposition] is in D minor and F major, with certain
> chromatic nuances, nuances it is true, that many people take for modulations.
> It is neither necessary nor indeed suitable to include a large number of
> modulations in this first reprise. To begin with, the models that the great
> masters have left us contain very few. Moreover, the powerful resources of
> modulation and sudden transition must be reserved for the second part of a
> large movement; this is because [the development] consists solely of trans-
> posed repetitions of themes ('chants') taken from the [exposition], and above
> all because the fullest resources must be brought into play there and attempts
> made to stir the profoundest emotions. [p. 332]... It is especially in the
> [development] that a good composer will reveal himself. It is there above all
> that genius has need of the support of science [viz. knowledge]. The richest

harmony, the profoundest counterpoint, indeed everything unexpected and entrancing in the magic art of transition must be developed there. [p. 387]

Nor does Momigny's interest in the expressive potential of harmony stop here. His K421 commentary is full of penetrating and detailed observation: he remarks upon the 'cruel dissonance' of 31–2; the extraordinary opening of the [development]; the tonal ambiguity in bars 43–4; and the enharmonic modulation to A minor in 45–6, 'a sombre utterance that penetrates the very depths of the soul'; he admires Mozart's interrupted cadences, especially at bar 14 ('un cri, une interjection') and – more simply – at bar 26, a 'delightful' way of extending a 'lovely and elegant phrase' (p. 377). He is aware, too, of Mozart's skill in subtly varying and balancing the harmonies of repeated phrases:

Why [he asks] did not the great Mozart place under the first [phrase] (1–4) the chromatic chords that are in the second (5–8)? Because when the same melody is repeated with a different harmony the diatonic chords must come first ... for if they are heard after the chromatic chords (which are naturally more piquant) they will seem insipid. [p. 373]

Momigny was equally alive to the expressive qualities of texture.

Anything that the principal character – the melody – cannot express, even with the help of words, the accompaniment will help to express. It may in its way suggest the scene setting ... It will above all depict the situation in which the actor finds himself: his calmness, his agitation, his anger, his grief, his delight, his sadness, his joy, his indifference, his love or his hate [p. 374]

There are many such places in the D minor Quartet to which Momigny draws attention: the 'sighing' cello line of bars 54–5; the first violin counter-subject ('si expressif, cet élan de l'ame'); the heightened intensity of the scoring of bars 11–12, which mirror 9–10 ('Fidèle à la gradation, Mozart l'observe ici on ne peut mieux'). Momigny is sensitive, too, to the tightly woven thematic structure – to the ways in which Mozart unifies without at the same time 'overrepeating' himself (how for instance, at bar 63 he avoids a third repetition 'qui serait un défaut', and at the same time introduces an abbreviated form of the first subject). He spots, too, many smaller figures that serve to tighten up the structure: the firm cello line beneath the [second subject]; the dotted crotchet/quaver figure derived from the [first subject], again in the cello, that underpins the development between bars 59 and 65.

The most significant part of Momigny's commentary is written from the standpoint of the orator – or perhaps more to the point, of the opera-goer, for it was in the opera house that late eighteenth-century audiences experienced great music most frequently and most powerfully. Momigny thus thought of an instrumental composition (and particularly the highly dramatic first movement of Mozart's D minor Quartet) as a wordless operatic aria, having a grammatical structure and a programme of its own.

The fullest description of grammatical structure is to be found on pp. 397–8 of the *Cours complet*. Momigny identifies three principal units in first movement form: the *reprise* (described above), the *période* and the *vers*. There are also further subdivisions into *phrases*, *propositions* (or *cadences*) and *membres*: the entire vocabulary is literary in terminology. Momigny's piano reduction of the [exposition] sets out the structure clearly enough (see Example 80 below).[4] Each of the seven periods encompasses a distinct unit: we would probably describe the first two periods as the first group, (a) and (b); the third and fourth as the transition; the fifth as the second group; and the last two as codetta motives. Momigny suggests that the *périodes* are of three kinds: *périodes capitales*, *périodes intermédiaires* and *périodes inférieures*. He identifies four types of *période capitale*, and in doing so shows a particular preoccupation with the idea of mood contrast. Two of the four are what would now be called the first and second subjects: the *période de début* and the *période mélodieuse* (see the Haydn analysis below). The other two *périodes capitales* comprise materials that according to modern theory are of subsidiary importance: the *période de verve* and the *trait*. The *période de verve* (Haydn, Symphony No. 103, bars 48–59) is normally full of energy and comes between the *période de début* and a quiet *période intermédiaire*: the other – the *trait* – is the vehicle for instrumental virtuosity, and is designed as a contrast with the surrounding periods. Momigny identifies two kinds of *période inférieure*: the *période conjonctionelle* (Mozart bars 67–9) that serves to bind two *périodes capitales* together; and the *période complémentaire* (Mozart, bars 32–5) that serves to round off another *période*. *Périodes intermédiaires* (Mozart, bars 8–14 and 14–20) are placed between *périodes capitales* and can be of either a thematic or a transitional character.

Each period comprises a number of interlocking verses. In the first period there are two verses, the second mirroring the first and balancing it in such a way that the home key of D minor is firmly established. In the second period the verses are much shorter: Momigny suggests that there are no less than six verses in all (it could equally well be argued that there are just two, the binding figure or *lien* being part of the main verse). In the third period Momigny identifies three verses, the first of which (the ninth) is divided by a rest into two *hémistiches* ... and so on. Academic as all this may sound, it has the function of drawing the reader's attention to the various levels of phrase structure within the movement. Mozart's slurrings articulate the individual figures, as indeed do the slurrings in baroque music; cadence, melody and texture together combine to form larger units that the actual notation does not define. Momigny's awareness of these larger units is clear enough, and it is one to which we can readily respond.

To bring the analysis alive to the ordinary reader, Momigny devised

**Ex. 80**  Mozart, String Quartet K421, as presented by Momigny

Ex. 80   *(cont.)*

Ex. 80   (cont.)

programmes for both the E flat Symphony and the D minor Quartet, just as E. T. A. Hoffmann was to do in his Beethoven analyses. Momigny's scheme for the quartet is particularly elaborate, and it well repays close study:

> The style of this *Allegro moderato* is noble and full of pathos. I believe that the best way to make my readers aware of its true quality is to set words to it. Since these verses (if indeed they may be called verses) are as it were 'improvised', they should only be judged in relation to the spirit of the music to which they are set. The feelings expressed by the composer are to be imagined as those of the beloved who is on the point of being deserted by her hero. Dido ... immediately sprang to mind. The nobility of her rank, the warmth of her love, the greatness of her misfortune, all these persuaded me to make her the heroine of this piece.

In reading through the simple text that Momigny has fitted to the music we should recall that Aeneas has been commanded by the Gods to set sail from Carthage. To his distress he has been forbidden to explain to his beloved Dido why he must go. She, in ignorance, is torn between feelings of anger at his apparent faithlessness, self pity and a desire that he should stay. The point here is not, of course, the literal story, but the emotional framework that Momigny perceived in the music. His arrangement takes the form of an aria for solo soprano [violin] – for convenience he gives the accompanying parts in piano reduction. He also provides a full score of Mozart's original, together with additional analytical staves of the exposition, showing the music's melodic and harmonic structure (see Example 80).

[Exposition]
1st period:  Ah! when you are the cause of my displeasure, ungrateful one, I want to pity myself, and not to soften your heart: bar 2. 1st Vn – This part of the *période de début* seems to me sublime (402); the 2nd Vn/ viola figure expresses the grief that Dido feels. (1–8)

2nd period:  What! You can leave me without blushing? What, can nothing prevent you? (8–14)

3rd period:  Go! ... No stay, yes stay, or I will die. – Dido, mindful of nothing but her indignation, says Go! But her ardent love, and the hope of touching her hero immediately bring back to her the situation in which she is placed. (14–18)

4th period:  I plead with you; if I lose you I will die! (18–24)

5th period:  Ah! If Dido has ever had any charms for you, don't look on her without pity, she whose tears are flowing. (24–32)

6th period:  Be sensible to my misfortunes. (32–37)

7th period:  Instrumental music only (Aeneas does not respond) (37–39)

8th period:  What! You do not reply? (39–41)

[Development]
1st period:  Alas! My tears, my beauty, they do not touch you. You wish to kill me. Monster, unworthy of the day, this is the reward for so much

love! How [violently] the indignation of the Queen of Carthage
bursts out in the music of the third verse! And how fittingly the
last syllable of the word *amour* is placed on the B flat to express the
grief that Dido feels . . .! The second time she tries to say the word,
she is overcome with mortification (bars 42–52).

2nd period:  Be gone, you wretch! (53–59)
3rd period:  No, stay yet; (in an aside: he seems to be moved). (59–63)
4th period:  To the one who adores you, give life and happiness; (63–66)
4th period, *complément*: no, tear apart my heart, ungrateful one! (66–67)
5th period:  Yes, tear apart my heart, ungrateful one! (67–69)
[Recapitulation] (70–   )
as Exposition: but final coda (112–end) has, 'I can no longer endure your
hardheartedness.'

In this combined poetic and technical analysis there is little that escapes
Momigny's critical eye and little with which we would choose to quarrel.
Perhaps not all the analytical detail is fully thought out; oddly, for instance,
Momigny places the start of the fourth *période* at bar 20, though this is merely
a continuation of the material that emerges in the upbeat to bar 19. Curious-
ly, too, there are discrepancies between the *période* structures of the exposition and the recapitulation. The importance of the analysis is nonetheless
twofold: it starts from the assumption that the form is *binary*, a fact that is
insufficiently appreciated today; most significantly of all, however, it treats
the whole as a dramatic entity, serving to remind us of the important role
that opera played in the forming of the classical style – an operatic world very
far removed from the world of Handel and Bach.

# 9

## Leopold Mozart and the K421 String Quartet

Young Wolfgang must have learned a great deal from his father, in the fields of both performance and composition, for Leopold Mozart was an experienced teacher and a devoted father. There was, for instance, that priceless art of relaxed concentration in performance, which Wolfgang so vividly describes in a letter to his father, dated 28 April 1784:

> I must write this in a hurry. Herr Richter, the clavier player, is making a tour on his way back to Holland, his native country ... He plays well as far as execution goes, but you will discover when you hear him that he is too rough and laboured, and entirely lacking in taste and feeling ... When I played to him he stared all the time at my fingers and kept on saying, 'Good God! How hard I work and sweat ... and to you, my friend, it is all child's play.' 'Yes', I replied, 'I too had to work hard so as not to have to work hard any longer.'[1]

Leopold's constant concern for expressive playing, too, must have got into his son's bones at a very early stage. Wolfgang certainly had nothing but contempt for mechanical virtuosity. In a letter of 7 June 1783:

> Well, I have a few words to say to my sister about Clementi's sonatas. Everyone who plays them or listens to them must feel that they are worthless. They contain no remarkable or striking passages save those in sixths and octaves. And I implore her not to practice these too much, so that she may not spoil her quiet, even touch, and that her hand may not lose its natural lightness, flexibility and smooth rapidity ... Supposing you do play sixths and octaves with the utmost velocity (which no one can do, not even Clementi) you only produce an atrocious chopping effect and nothing else whatever. Clementi is a *ciarlatano* like all Italians ... He has not the slightest expression or taste, still less, feeling.

Today we are indebted to Leopold above all for his *Violinschule*, which is of interest not only as a technical book about violin playing, but as a major source of information about mid eighteenth-century performance practice.[2] Its origins go back to 1743, when Leopold entered the service of the

Archbishop of Salzburg as a violinist. Within a year he had become violin teacher to the Archbishop's choristers. Finding that none of the available books on violin playing were at all satisfactory, he began to develop his own method. It was only after Quantz and C. P. E. Bach had published their flute and keyboard tutors in the early 1750s, however, that he decided to go into print, encouraged by the Berlin critic F. W. Marpurg. At first the book was barely a modest success. By 1766, however, its value was being increasingly recognised. By 1800 it had been through four German editions, as well as one in Dutch and one in French. Several later violin tutors were based upon it.

To learn from it how the violin and bow were held is to discover a great deal about the way in which an eighteenth-century performance would have been projected. To read Leopold's comments on bowing – whether or not one is a violinist – is to find out much about phrasing, articulation and dynamics. To study his system of fingering is to study eighteenth-century concepts of phrasing and tone colour. Throughout the book, too, there are invaluable clues about expressive performance, notably about rhythmic flexibility, which involves an awareness of the 'good' and 'bad' notes within each phrase (see above, p. 14).

## LEOPOLD MOZART'S TREATISE

### Posture and bow control

The very first point to note is Leopold's concern to develop a 'singing' style of performance. Although Leopold favoured a 'strong, masculine bow stroke', this must be seen in the context of the frontispiece illustration, where the violin is pictured *resting* on the shoulder (there is no chin rest with which to grip the instrument) and the bowing arm hangs relaxedly against the side. Leopold's recommendations on relaxed posture in fact reveal much about the kind of unforced, singing style that he had in mind.

Leopold considered bowing to be the single most important aspect of violin playing. It is bowing, he said, that 'gives life to the notes' (chap. VII, section 1, para. 1). It is hardly surprising, then, that many of his most valuable hints on performance practice are to be found in the extensive chapters on bowing. The chapter on bow control begins with a series of exercises in the playing of a single sustained note. The first one asks for a crescendo from the heel to the middle of the bow and a diminuendo from the middle to the tip (a *messa di voce*). The next exercise is to produce a gradual diminuendo from heel to tip of the bow, and so on, until every gradation of dynamics has been rehearsed in every part of the bow, extending to six or more crescendi and diminuendi per stroke. Players at this time then, were encouraged to develop great sensitivity to dynamic nuance. Leopold particularly warned against forcing the tone (V/13 and XII/16), as did C. P. E. Bach in his keyboard book.

Fortissimos are no more appropriate for the music of Mozart's day than they had been for the music of Bach and Handel.

The basis of Leopold's bowing system was still the 'rule of the downbow', a rule that has been discussed in the contexts of French, Italian and German baroque string techniques (see above, p. 26). The simple applications of the rule are discussed at length in the very first technical chapter of the book (chapter four), and there are many examples such as those given in Example 81 below to illustrate the argument.

**Ex. 81**    Leopold Mozart: some illustrations of the downbow principle

Having set out the basic principles, Leopold went on in chapter seven to show how the system could be developed to meet the demands of contemporary music. No reputable singer, he declared, would stop for breath during the course of a phrase or chop a legato melodic line into pieces. Just as the voice 'glides' naturally from one note to the next, so the violinist should aim for a 'natural', singing style of performance and thus for a bowing technique that is able 'to fit many notes into one bow stroke'. In earlier times, of course, the normal procedure had been to bow each note separately, though baroque virtuosi had learned how to fit astonishingly large numbers of notes into a single bow-stroke.

Perhaps the single most important point to emerge from this chapter – at least as far as the general reader is concerned – is that bowing slurs tell us a good deal about rhythm, accentuation and phrasing. Nowadays the slur has two rather different functions. It can be used (as it was then) to indicate a bowing or a tonguing, in which case it will normally cover no more than a dozen notes at the most. It can also be used, however, to mark out a long-term phrase of several bars, during the course of which there may be several bowings or tonguings. This second type of slur only gradually emerged. There are very few 'phrasing' slurs in classical or early romantic music; few eighteenth-century slurs even cross the barline, for when a continuous legato was required, each complete bar would be bowed separately. This notational convention was still alive when Czerny published his *Royal Pianoforte School* in 1839 (see Example 82).

**Ex. 82**   Czerny's continuous slurring

> When slurs are drawn over several notes [he wrote], although they are not continuous but are broken into several lines, they are considered as forming but one, and no perceptible separation must take place. [Vol. I: lesson 18, para. 24]

One further point needs to be underlined in connection with slurring: Leopold's concern that the *expressive* quality of the slur be brought out. The short slur was not just a technical convenience; it was something to be heard. The first note of a slur was to be held 'a little long'; the slur thus shaped the flow of the music, imparting to it a subtle give-and-take that is the hallmark of a musical performance. According to the first example in the chapter, for instance, patterns of four slurred semiquavers should be played in such a way that the first semiquaver of each four is gently stressed and 'marked with a vigour that inspires the whole performance'. Of all the slurring patterns, pairs of semiquavers are the commonest, the first note being held 'a little long', the second being played, therefore, rather late, and quietly. Some of Leopold's many different slurrings are illustrated in Example 83.

Slurrings are part of that wider aspect of musical rhythm about which Mozart wrote in letters to his father of 23 and 24 October 1777:

> What these people cannot grasp is that in tempo rubato in an Adagio, the left hand should go on playing in strict time. With them the left hand always follows suit.

**Ex. 83**    Leopold Mozart: some alternative bowings of a melody

It is a question of balancing rhythm against metre [Couperin's *mésure* being tempered by *cadence*]. A proper balance cannot of course be achieved until the player has acquired a fine sense of timing. Mozart considered this to be the chief requisite of performance, and one that was most difficult to develop.

Mozart's subtle and extensive slurrings in the K421 Quartet provide an ideal model for study. The very first phrase contains within it two problems (see Example 84). Although the shape of the first violin line would seem to call for a downbow on the first beat of the third bar, an upbow is inevitable if Mozart's previous slurrings are respected. Is this, then, Mozart's way of avoiding what might otherwise become a melodramatic accentuation of the falling seventh on that first beat? The second problem concerns the cello. Multi-bar bowings are exceptional in the music of this period. Why, then, did Mozart choose to bow together the first three bars, rather than to use the normal bar-by-bar notation? Is this in fact a precursor of the nineteenth-century phrase mark, or is Mozart really asking for a single bow stroke? Had the dynamic marking been 'sotto voce' each time the phrase recurs, the second answer might have seemed appropriate. However, as the marking is *f* at the beginning of the development, Mozart is evidently underlining the

**Ex. 84**  Mozart, String Quartet K421: Allegro

need for a total legato between bars 42 and 44, even though the minims are probably going to be bowed in groups of two.[3]

There are many places where Mozart's directions are at odds with modern bowing practices. Take, for instance, the remarkable transition in bars 14–24 that simply grows and grows as it moves upwards (Example 85). There is such a feeling of inexorable expansion through bars 15–18 that there is a danger of starting the crescendo too early, and of overdoing it. Has Mozart allowed the first and second violins in bar 17 sufficient bow for the desired expression? Or is the bowing again underlining the fact that the entire passage is based on a *piano* dynamic? Mozart has slurred the textures of this passage so subtly, giving each line a characteristic of its own, that his

**Ex. 85**  Mozart, String Quartet K421: Allegro (bars 14–18)

markings should be changed only as a last resort. There are, of course, different ways of approaching these markings. There are places in the first movement where the 'period' choice of bow direction will feel somewhat strange to modern players – as, for instance, in bars 12–14 of the first movement.

**Ex. 86**  Implied bowings for the opening of Mozart's String Quartet K421

If any alterations are to be made to the slurring of the first movement, the first violin markings in bars 65 and 86–7 are perhaps the most obvious candidates for attention (after all, to deny that a composer may occasionally have erred would be to deny his humanity!). During the two bars before 65 there has been a steady crescendo which reaches *forte* on the third beat of 65. This is best achieved, perhaps, by taking a second bow on the third beat of the bar. The second passage, though parallel to that of 17–18, may be too complex to be satisfactorily managed in one bow. Before any change is made, however, the original must be given a chance to work and its implications fully analysed.

During the course of chapter five Mozart refers in several places to the existence of a small if barely audible 'softness' at the beginning and end of every bow stroke. This observation has led in recent years to some curious attempts at 'authentic' string playing, every separately bowed note beginning and ending softly with a crescendo in the middle, like a vocal *messa di voce* (see above, p. 84). The *messa di voce*, however, was a special effect, only to be applied to certain long notes (chap. V, para. 4). Extensive use of it would completely destroy the singing style of performance which Mozart was so anxious to cultivate. To achieve this singing style, he in fact recommended that bow direction changes be made as imperceptibly as possible. Each new stroke was to be started 'with a certain moderation', so that even the strongest stroke 'brought the already vibrating string *quite imperceptibly* from one movement into another and different movement' (V/10). This, he emphasised, was what he meant by an initial softness. In no way should that softness be taken as an invitation to treat lyrical lines in a disconnected (and hence unvocal) manner.

Leopold was also concerned that the violinist should produce a consistently rounded tone, whatever the character of the music. Again he drew an analogy with voice production, the aim of which was an even and consistent quality of sound throughout the entire range (V/13). Open strings, therefore, were to be avoided, 'for they are too loud compared with stopped ones, and pierce the ear too sharply'. He also recommended that each self-contained phrase should be played on one string as far as possible, to ensure consistency of colour. 'A pleasing result is obtained owing to the equality of the tone' if, for instance, bars 4 (second beat) to 10 of the passage in Example 87 are all played on the A string (chap. VIII, sect. 3, para. 14).
Leopold was very conscious of the differences in tone that could be produced by varying the position of the bow on the string (V/11). Nowhere, though, did he discuss the expressive potential of this technique. His one concern was to ensure evenness of tone.

**Ex. 87** Leopold Mozart's fingerings

## Dynamics

Many smaller points of general interest emerge from Leopold's *Versuch*. There are, for instance, many hints on dynamics, the signs for which occur rather erratically in late eighteenth-century music. Leopold makes it amply clear that a good performance would have been subtly nuanced, whether or not there were detailed markings in the score. He suggested, for instance, that where there were no dynamic markings, long notes that were surrounded by shorter ones might be played *fp*. The second note of a slurred 1+3 pair might also be played 'with a sustained yet gradually decreasing tone' (VII/2/4). Notes that were sharpened during the course of a phrase were always to be played rather more strongly, the tone diminishing again during the course of the melody (XII/8). Similarly, notes that were suddenly flattened were to be marked by a *forte*, as in Example 88.

**Ex. 88** Leopold Mozart's dynamics

Upbeat 1+3 pairs were to be played so that the first note was less loud than the second, but without hurrying (VII/2/7). In playing the *sforzando*, Leopold recommended that the bow should remain on the string, the stroke continuing 'so that the sound continues, although *gradually* dying away' (XII/8, XII/12), just as the sound of a bell, when struck sharply, by degrees dies away' (I/3/18, fn 1).

The two commonly used *sforzando* markings were *fp* and *sfp*. In the D minor Quartet Mozart seems to be using *fp* to indicate a very short accentuation, for wherever he uses the *sfp* he separates the *sf* from the *p*, to suggest a more gradual fall back from the accent (see K302, Example 89). In other places, however, he seems, like Hummel to have used the two markings synonymously.

**Ex. 89**    Violin Sonata K302: first movement

The classical *sforzando* was probably less emphatic than it was later to become. It may be that the increasing use of the 'hairpin' parallels the change in the character of the *sforzando*. Czerny (see p. 192, n. 9) recommended that notes marked with a hairpin be given 'a slight degree of emphasis', though not as much as the next loudest dynamic would require. *Sf*, *fz* and *sfz*, however, were to be 'struck smartly and emphatically'. Obviously the musical context must determine the intensity of the accent: a *sforzando* in a quiet slow movement must surely be less pronounced than one in a vigorous presto.

Although Quantz mentions in his *Versuch* (IV/23) the technique of 'swelling' and 'diminishing' notes, Leopold Mozart was one of the first to define the terms 'crescendo' and 'diminuendo' (I/3/27). 'Crescendo,' he wrote, 'means increasing, and tells us that successive notes ... are to increase in tone throughout. Decrescendo, on the other hand, signifies that the volume of tone is to fade away more and more'. Clearly, however, subtle nuances were far more important to Leopold than broad dynamic contrasts, a fact that is underlined by his early insistence on the avoidance of aggressive loudness (V/13).

Wolfgang Mozart rarely used the term 'crescendo'; still less did he employ long, Mannheim-style crescendos of the kind to be found in the K320

'Posthorn' Serenata. He used 'decrescendo' and 'calando' very infrequently, and 'diminuendo' not at all. In later works especially, however, $f$ and $p$ signs often relate to each other in a way that implies a gradual dynamic change, since they are more spaced out from each other. One such instance is to be found in the K454 violin sonata (see Example 90).

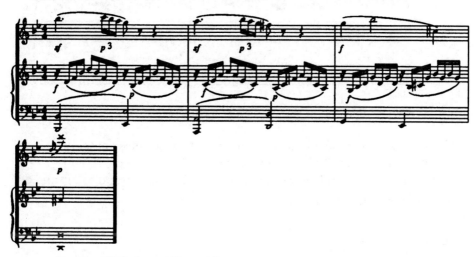

**Ex. 90**   Violin Sonata K454: Allegro

The dynamic markings in the K421 Quartet are unusually copious, and for the most part they are explicit. Since Mozart (uncharacteristically) uses the term 'crescendo' a good deal here, juxtapositions of $f$ and $p$ should probably be treated as dynamic contrasts, especially in the highly dramatic first movement. Even so, there may be one or two exceptions. In the tenth bar of the slow movement, for instance, players may feel more comfortable with a crescendo immediately before the $f$, and with a gentle crescendo in bars 12 (beat 5) and 13 (see Example 91).

**Ex. 91**   Dynamics in Mozart's String Quartet K421

**Ex. 92**    Dynamics in Mozart's String Quartet K421

There may, too, be a number of implied decrescendos, notably in bars 17–18, 42–6 and 87–8 of the first movement, bars 3–4, 17–18 and 51–2 of the slow movement and on the tied notes between bars 66 and 67, 67 and 68, 68 and 69 and 69 and 70 of the finale (Example 92).

CLASSICAL TEMPOS

Late eighteenth- and early nineteenth-century composers used a wide range of Italian terms, though usually in a relatively straightforward manner. Hummel and Czerny (see below, p. 175) give particularly clear accounts of them in their piano tutors (the order in which the terms are ranked below is theirs).

Table 4

| | |
|---|---|
| Grave | very slow, solemn, measured |
| Largo | nearly the same degree of slowness |
| Larghetto | not so slow, yet rather dragging |
| Lento | slow |
| Adagio | slow, but full of soul and expression (very slow, yet not dragging)[a] |
| Andantino | gently moving onwards (Hummel places this after Andante and gives 'progressing with a tolerably slow pace') |
| Andante | advancing, going forward |
| Allegretto | rather cheerful, light, pleasing (yet not hurrying) |
| Allegro | cheerful and lively (fast, with agility) |
| Vivacissimo | very lively and fiery (not in Hummel) |
| Presto | very lively and fiery (very fast and vivacious) |
| Prestissimo | as rapidly as possible. |

[a]Where there is disagreement between the two, Hummel's definition is given in brackets.

Mozart himself probably had no clear feeling for the difference between adagio and largo, and he qualified both in the direction of 'less slow', i.e.

larghetto, un poco adagio and adagio ma non troppo. He used largo rarely, though the qualified larghetto occurs a good deal. The commonest terms in classical scores are undoubtedly andante and allegro, both of which are often qualified: for instance, Mozart used such combinations as andante un poco adagio, andante con moto and allegro vivace. In such cases the speed implications are obvious enough. The fast extremes, presto and prestissimo, are rare. That Mozart was aware of the speed implications of alla breve is clear from his criticism of Clementi's playing in a letter written on 7 June 1783:

> Clementi is a *ciarlatano* [he declared], like all Italians! He puts presto at the beginning of a sonata – even prestissimo and alla breve – but he actually plays the music allegro in 4/4 time.

That Mozart enjoyed an exhilarating prestissimo can hardly be doubted, for after all, he directed the last movement of the 'Haffner' Symphony to be played 'as quickly as possible'! Under no circumstances, however, was speed to impair clarity, as we see in a letter dated 17 January 1778:

> It is much easier to play a piece quickly than slowly: in difficult passages one or two notes can be left out without anyone being the wiser. But is that beautiful? ... [A good performance is one in which] the piece is taken at the proper speed, and in which all the notes, appoggiaturas and so forth are played exactly as written and with the appropriate expression and taste, as if the composer himself were playing.

Mozart unexpectedly uses alla breve markings not only in fast movements but also in a large number of andante and larghetto movements, thereby reducing the normal number of 'good' (accented) beats per bar by half. Many of these alla breve time signatures have been altered in the old Breitkopf edition. The proper marking, for instance, for the lovely slow movement of the K595 Piano Concerto is 'Larghetto: Alla breve'. The omission of 'alla breve' could cause the player to adopt a fatally slow speed.[4] Vague though the Italian terms may be for tempo and mood, Mozart shows every sign of taking them seriously, as we shall see below, in connection with K421.

EDITIONS

Like his father, Wolfgang was keen that the composer's performance instructions should be meticulously observed. There was the case, for instance, of Miss Rosa Cannabich, whom Wolfgang was struggling to teach when he was at Mannheim in 1777:

> The Andante [he wrote to his mother on 16 November] will give us most trouble for it is full of expression and must be played accurately and with the exact shades of *forte* and *piano*, precisely as they are marked.[5]

Both father and son would certainly have welcomed the idea of the Urtext edition in which the composer's score is reproduced as faithfully as possible in modern notation. Unfortunately, as the Badura-Skodas have pointed out, there are a great many bad editions still in circulation, ranging from the downright imaginative (such as the late nineteenth-century Mozart editions of Riemann) to the apparently Urtext but wholly unreliable *Mozart Ausgabe* published between 1876 and 1886, which has been the basis for a number of later editions, including many of the Eulenberg miniature scores.[6]

Some editorial shortcomings are admittedly the result of Mozart's often hasty script. His rhythms and pitches are normally clear enough, but dynamics, slurs, dots and dashes are not always carefully drawn or consistently applied. When hurried, Mozart tended to begin a slur too soon on the page and to end it too late. Many of his dots look like dashes, and vice versa, raising the question as to whether he always intended to distinguish between the two.[7] Because of such deficiencies as these, editors tended until recently to allow themselves a very free hand with articulation markings and dynamics, fusing together successions of whole-bar slurs, and changing smaller slurs to fit their own ideas of how the music should be articulated, even when the composer's notation is crystal clear. The autograph score of the D minor Quartet is a case in point. It is clearly written, and its markings are consistently enough applied to discourage editorial intrusion. Even so, the old Peters edition (an excerpt is shown in Example 93), prepared 'partly from the first editions and partly from the setting of the compositions in Series 14 of the complete edition' (viz. Breitkopf and Härtel's 'critical' *Mozart Ausgabe* of 1878) differs from the original in many details.[8]

**Ex. 93**    A late nineteenth-century edition of Mozart's String Quartet K421

There can, for instance, be no argument about the slurring, in the autograph score, of the first violin part in the third and fourth bars (see Example 84 above) and in later equivalent bars (21 and 72), or about the slurring of the second violin in bars 4 and 73; in the ninth bar Mozart has purposely drawn the first four cello quavers in such a way as to make room for the *p* beneath the second quaver – and yet the editor has chosen to alter the originals without so much as a word. Many other dynamic markings are incorrectly placed: the *p* in second violin, viola and cello should be on the fourth beat of bar 23, for instance; early on in the development (bars 46–9), neither slurrings nor crescendos are marked in the score – and so on. In the first movement alone there are almost a hundred unexplained differences between the old Peters edition and Mozart's autograph score. Some of the variants are taken from the first edition of the printed parts, to be sure, but as there is no guarantee that the parts represent Mozart's second thoughts, or that the composer looked through the proofs of the parts, the modern reader has a right to know what the editor has done! A good modern edition, moreover, ought to alert the reader to any significant changes that the composer may have made in his score. Mozart was somewhat undecided, for instance, about the speeds of the outer movements; originally he headed the first movement 'Allegro moderato', but subsequently he crossed out the 'moderato'. Against the last movement he originally wrote 'Allegretto'; he then altered this to 'Andante', finally deciding upon 'Allegretto ma non troppo'. The reader should also be told that instead of simple turns in bars 24 and 93, Mozart wrote out the ornaments in full: in the first case the lower note B is altered to B natural; in the second, the G is not sharpened. Information of this kind can be particularly revealing, and it should not be withheld. If, therefore, an old edition has to be used in performance, it should be rigorously checked against a reliable modern Urtext.

### THE PROBLEM OF CLASSICAL ORNAMENTATION

Here it is necessary to cast the net rather wider than the study of K421 will allow, since it is particularly in the sphere of keyboard music that the full repertory of ornamentation flourished. It may be helpful, too, to attempt a comparison between Leopold Mozart's painstaking observations, set down in the *Versuch*, and Wolfgang's observed practice, if only to underline the fact that ornamentation has always been a living, personal thing, inviting interpretation rather than slavish copy. This point was well made in 1702 by Andreas Werckmeister[9], when he observed that most ornaments had a lifespan of no more than twenty or thirty years before they became old-fashioned and were dropped. No wonder, then, that late eighteenth-century ornamentation displayed some very unbaroque features, and that early nineteenth-century ornamentation was again something different.

As we have seen (p. 41 above), there were two principal types of baroque ornamentation: Italian improvised ornament, in which the player had a very free hand to decorate slowly moving lines; and French symbol notation, which indicated the note to be ornamented and its general shape, though not its precise detail. The classical conventions of ornamentation that Leopold Mozart discussed are in many ways an abbreviation and fusion of the French and Italian systems. According to him, the composer would normally indicate which notes were to be ornamented and in what manner. The player, for his part, interpreted the ornaments much more freely than in the past. For example, the ascending appoggiatura could be 'improved' by adding auxiliary notes, as in Example 94 (IX/10), whilst the simple trill could be turned into a veritable cadenza (X/5, 6).

**Ex. 94**   Leopold Mozart: improvised ornamentation

Leopold discussed ornamentation under three main headings: single-note ornaments (IX), trills (X) and mordents (XI). In this last chapter he also included a number of other freely improvised ornaments, such as the *ribbatuta*, the *Überwurf*, and the *Zurückschlag*, which the player could freely introduce at appropriate points in the music, after the old Italian manner (XI/17–19). Some of these are shown in Example 95.

as written

the circle, up and down

as written

the half-circle

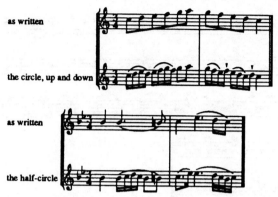

**Ex. 95**   Leopold Mozart: further suggestions for improvised ornamentation

For the performer today, Leopold Mozart's chapters on ornamentation have one important message: that in his day ornamentation was still very much more an art than a science. The speed, duration, articulation and weight of an ornament depended on the character of the music and on the precise context of the ornament itself. If the ornament sounded laboured or out of context, it quite simply was wrong. Leopold's 'rules', then, are no more than guidelines: a basis for action, rather than a precise set of instructions. They may be summarised as follows:

## Appoggiaturas

These are indicated by small notes; they normally take half the value of the note against which they are placed and are *always* slurred to it. The two figures shown in Example 96 are not, therefore, identical.

*a, written and played*                    *b, as written*                    *b, as played*

**Ex. 96**   The significance of the single grace note

In the first case all the semiquavers are equal; in the second, the first note is slurred to the second, whether or not a slur is given, and it is gently accented, the second note being played with a 'softer tone' (IX/3). Appoggiaturas on dotted notes take up two thirds of the value of the principal note, whilst appoggiaturas against minims and longer notes may last for three quarters of their value (IX/4, 5). According to Leopold, small notes were used to prevent further ornaments from being improvised on them.

He also gives examples of unaccented passing-notes that take their value, not from the following note, but from the previous one, as in Example 97 (IX/18). Badura-Skoda observes that Leopold Mozart was the first to document this usage, though it has some resemblance to the earlier French

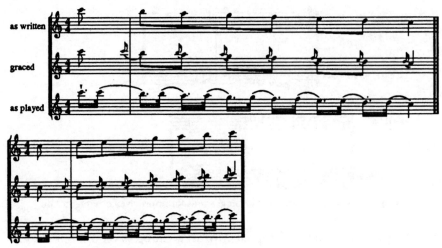

**Ex. 97**    Leopold Mozart: passing appoggiaturas

*tierce coulée*. In such cases the accent must fall on the main note and not on the appoggiatura. Leopold recommended, however, that such figures be written out fully to avoid confusion, a recommendation that Wolfgang certainly followed. Leopold concluded the section on the basic appoggiatura by suggesting ways in which it could be ornamented (IX/19, 22, 26, and 27).

### Trills

The easiest of Leopold's three chapters on ornamentation is the tenth, dealing with the trill. Three ways of beginning and three ways of ending the long trill are described, though the same trill sign is used for all of them. The trill could begin (i) immediately on the upper note; (ii) on an upper appoggiatura, thus holding the first note somewhat longer than (i); or (iii) ornamentally from below. The trill could end (i) simply and 'naturally' with a small note anticipating the note of resolution; (ii) with a small turn; or (iii) with an embellishment (X/5, 6). Some possibilities are shown in Example 98. Short trills were always to be played with a quick appoggiatura and a

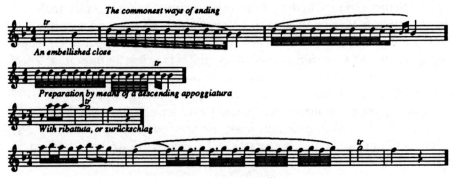

**Ex. 98**    Leopold Mozart: ways of playing trills

turn. The speed of the trill depended on the mood of the music. Trills could be accelerated, beginning softly and gradually getting louder as the speed increased, especially in cadenzas.

### Leopold Mozart's other ornaments

Leopold admitted that most people would recognise only one of his three mordent figures as a proper mordent. He argued, however, that all have a similar effect, the small notes being played as rapidly as possible, with the accent falling not on the ornament but on the main note. All mordents covered the interval of a semitone, the extended mordent or *battement* beginning a semitone below the main note (XI/9) (see Example 99).

**Ex. 99**    Leopold Mozart: mordents

### The vibrato

Significantly enough, Leopold considered vibrato to be a branch of ornamentation – and only a very minor branch, to judge from the little space that he devoted to it!

> [The vibrato] arises from nature herself ... for if we strike a slack string or a bell sharply we hear, after the stroke, a certain wave-like undulation of the struck note. [It] can be used charmingly on a long note, not only by good instrumentalists but also by skilful singers [XI/3].

He warned against the overuse of vibrato, observing that there were players who trembled continuously on every note 'as if they had the palsy'. Vibrato was only to be used where nature herself would produce it ... namely on long notes at the ends of phrases (XI/3). Then, as now, opinions differed as to just how much vibrato should be used. Mozart's distinguished contemporary Francesco Geminiani, for instance, probably used a great deal more vibrato than Leopold Mozart did:

> When it is long continued [Geminiani wrote], swelling the sound by degrees, drawing the bow nearer the bridge ... it may express Majesty, Dignity, etc. But making it shorter, lower and softer, it may denote Affliction, Fear, etc., and when it is made on short Notes, it only contributes to make their sound more agreeable, and for this reason, it should be made use of as often as possible.[10]

### WOLFGANG AMADEUS MOZART'S ORNAMENTATION

Wolfgang's ornamentation is a good deal more straightforward than his father's,[11] and while it should be viewed in the light of the principles that

Leopold enumerates, it should in no way be circumscribed by them. By far the commonest ornaments in Wolfgang's music are single-note appoggiaturas and trills. There are practically no mordents. Turns are comparatively rare, and they are relatively uncomplicated.

### Appoggiatura-type ornaments

To begin with, there is the question of just how seriously to take Mozart's apparently careful notation. Leopold stressed that appoggiatura notes are *always* slurred to their main notes. On the surface, then, Wolfgang had no need to slur appoggiatura pairs, and yet he often did. Leopold bluntly stated that appoggiaturas attached to minims, crotchets and quavers always took half the value of the main notes. In certain places, however, Wolfgang seems to be intending something else by varying the value of the small appoggiatura note: the principal figure of the Minuet of the K304 Violin Sonata, for example, contains a quaver appoggiatura, whilst the contrasting figure at bar 13 is written as a semiquaver, as if it is to be played more snappily (see Example 100).

**Ex. 100**    Violin Sonata K304: Tempo di Minuetto

Mozart's meaning here is by no means clear. In the Piano Sonata K283 (see Example 101), the semiquaver appoggiaturas invite different interpretations: the first, in bar 54, is a snappy 3+1, whereas in bar 59, the ornament surely occupies half the main note – a semiquaver.

**Ex. 101**    Piano Sonata K283: Allegro

The well-known opening of the A minor Piano Sonata K310 (Example 102) presents the player with a similar problem. The two appoggiaturas in the first two bars look identical, and yet they could well be played differently, the first snappily (on account of the dissonant sharpened fourth), the second smoothly, as two equal quavers (because it has very much the quality of a conventional cadential suspension). No set of rules, then, can possibly cover every situation.

Ex. 102    Piano Sonata K310: Allegro maestoso

All the single-note ornaments in the K421 Quartet are clearly marked in the autograph score as acciaccaturas (see Example 103).

Ex. 103    Acciaccaturas in Mozart's String Quartet K421

Leopold implied that appoggiaturas should be played on the beat. The only certain cases of appoggiaturas to be played before the beat in Wolfgang's music are fully written out, as in the A major Symphony K201. There are countless appoggiaturas, however, that must be treated as acciaccaturas if they are to be played on the beat, the small note being played as quickly as possible. A case in point is the Allegro alla Turca from the K331 Piano Sonata, bars 107 and 114. The ornaments here are identical to the one in bar 65; in bars 107 and 114 there is a strong case for interpreting the signs as acciaccaturas, though in bars 64–7 an appoggiatura would seem to be more appropriate (Example 104).

Ex. 104   Piano Sonata K331: Rondo alla Turca

An acciaccatura-like interpretation, too, seems very apt for fast-moving, staccato contexts like that shown in Example 105.

Ex. 105   Violin Sonata K305: Allegro di molto

In the passage from the first movement of the K281 Piano Sonata shown in Example 106, the appoggiaturas have to be played on the beat, simply because there is no time for them earlier (this goes, too, for the appoggiatura-like figure in bar 102).

Ex. 106   Piano Sonata K281: Allegro

On the other hand, the vertical alignment of the *forte* chords in the Presto of the K280 Piano Sonata make the placement of the appoggiaturas before the beat almost unavoidable (Example 107).

Ex. 107   Piano Sonata K280: Presto

So far, appoggiaturas have only been considered in relation to undotted crotchets, quavers and semiquavers. Dotted notes and longer notes raise additional problems. Leopold ruled that such appoggiaturas should take up two thirds or three quarters of the value of the main notes to which they were attached. The rigid application of this rule to Wolfgang's music will produce odd results in places. Once again, the player must decide what is appropriate, taking into account the character of the music, and especially the context in which the ornament is set (see Examples 108 and 109).

**Ex. 108**    Piano Sonata K332: Allegro assai

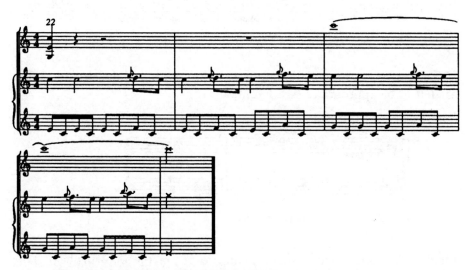

**Ex. 109**    Violin Sonata K296: Allegro vivace

*Trills*

According to Leopold, the trill could be interpreted in many different ways. There is no reason to suppose that Wolfgang would have been any stricter than his father in this respect. In the absence of evidence to the contrary, all but very elaborate cadential trills should normally start on the upper note. This note may be held if desired, in the manner of an appoggiatura, whether or not it is actually written out, as it is in the K7 violin sonata (see Example 110).

**Ex. 110**    Violin Sonata K7: Adagio

Wolfgang frequently indicated the addition of a turn at the end of a long trill, as in Example 111.

**Ex. 111**    Piano Sonata K570: Allegretto

The absence of a turn should not prevent its addition, if the circumstances are felt to be appropriate (see Example 112).

**Ex. 112**    Piano Sonata K533: Allegretto

On the other hand, a short trill may end abruptly on the following beat, if the circumstances seem right (see Example 113).

**Ex. 113**   Piano Sonata K283: Allegro

In the K421 Quartet, the first subject trill, which plays such an important part in the first movement, could continue into the following note, stop on the second quaver, or be even shorter. Its treatment could vary, too, depending on its context – it could be at its shortest, for instance, during the dramatic early part of the development.

Some of Mozart's shorter trills pose particular problems. In the eleventh variation of the K284 Piano Sonata, for instance, there is hardly time to play the demisemiquaver, let alone its trill, even though the tempo marking is Adagio cantabile (Example 114).

**Ex. 114**   Piano Sonata K284: Variation XI, Adagio cantabile

Either the trill must be reduced to G–A–G (beginning, that is, on the main note), or it must be started marginally before the beat. Short trills in fast-moving music must similarly be curtailed, as in the entirely typical passage from the K284 Piano Sonata shown in Example 115.

**Ex. 115**   Piano Sonata K284: Allegro con spirito

### Other ornaments

Wolfgang's other ornaments are quite straightforward. Groups of two or three small notes, acting like appoggiaturas, must be interpreted in ways appropriate to the context, as above. Turns should be played as four-note figures, the only problem being their placing. In the K457 Sonata there is only room to play the turn on the demisemiquaver beat. In the Andante of the K533 Sonata, on the other hand, the turn could start on the second semiquaver. In bar 22 of the K475 Fantasia, however, it could well be held back until the third semiquaver, since Mozart here has gone to the unusual lengths of notating a double-dotted rhythm (see Example 116).

Ex. 116   Piano Sonatas K457 and 533; Fantasy K475

The fully written out turns in the finale of the K421 Quartet present no particular problems and perhaps sound their best when played in such a way as to underline the strong rhythmic flow of the music (see Example 117).

Ex. 117   Mozart's written-out turn, K421

# Haydn's 'Drum Roll' Symphony in E flat No. 103

## THE CLASSICAL ORCHESTRA

By the time Haydn came to write his last six symphonies for the London impresario and violinist/conductor Johann Peter Salomon he was universally respected as one of the two greatest composers of the time. His music formed the backbone of orchestral concerts everywhere – Paris, London, Leipzig, Hamburg, Vienna and a hundred smaller cities and courts where music was treasured. It is impossible to generalise about the numerous orchestras that would have played his music. Some, like the Esterház ensemble of the 1770s, were little more than chamber groups, the string section numbering no more than a dozen players. More string players were engaged at Esterház during the 1770s, but at no time does the number seem to have exceeded twenty. At the first performance of the 'Drum Roll' Symphony in London, however, Haydn presided over an orchestra of more than sixty players. Once again, small was not necessarily seen as beautiful (see Corelli, above, p. 80).

As the table below shows, the average orchestral string group numbered between twenty and forty, though larger groups were assembled from time to time: the strings of the 1781 Vienna orchestra numbered 68, for instance, four more than Mahler's Vienna Philharmonic Orchestra of 1900, whilst no fewer than 79 strings were engaged for one of Beethoven's Vienna concerts in 1814! Orchestral standards varied a good deal, as might be expected. Haydn's early Esterház orchestra was probably little better than mediocre, comprising as it did players who were by no means exclusively professional musicians. On the other hand, Haydn's London 'Drum Roll' orchestra was led by no less a distinguished figure than the celebrated soloist and teacher G. B. Viotti. In Haydn's day the orchestra was directed either from the leading desk of the first violins or from a keyboard instrument placed in the centre of the ensemble. When he came to London in 1793 Haydn is reported to have conducted from a fortepiano. When Mozart played his piano concer-

Table 5[1]. Some European orchestras in the late eighteenth-century[a]

| | | |
|---|---|---|
| Galeazzi[2]: | (a) 2, 2, 1, 1, –/ | |
| | (b) 6, 6, 3, 2, 2/ | |
| | (c) 26,26,10,6, 6/ | |

*London*
| 1776 | 8, 8, 5,4, 2/ 4,–,–,4 |
|---|---|
| 1791 | 16 . . , 4,4, 4/ 2,2,–,2 |
| 1795 | 12,12, 5,6, 5/ 4,4,4,4 |

*Mannheim*
| 1756 | 10,10, 4,4, 2/ 4,2,–,2 (court) |
|---|---|
| 1782 | 25 . . . , 3,4, 3/ 4,3,4,4 (court) |

*Esterház*
| 1774 | 3, 3, 2,1, 1/ 1,2,–,2 (court) |
|---|---|
| 1783 | 10 . . , 2,2, 2/ –,2,–,2 (court) |

*Vienna*
| 1781 | 6, 6, 4, 3, 3/ 2,2,2,2 (opera) |
|---|---|
| 1781 | 20,20,10, 8,10/ 4,4,4,6 |
| 1782 | 6, 6, 4, 3, 3/ 2,2,–,2 (court) |
| 1813 | 8 . . . , 2, 2, 2/ 2,2,2,2 |
| 1814 | 36 . . ,14,12,17/ 2,2,2,2 |

*Berlin*
| 1754 | 12 . . . , 4, 4, 2/ 4,3,–,4 (court) |
|---|---|
| 1792 | 11,11, 7, 8 4/ 4,5,2,5 (court) |

*Paris*
| 1778 | 22 . . . , 6, 9, 6/ 2,2,2,2 |
|---|---|
| 1790 | 13,13, 6,12, 5/ 2,4,2,5 (opera) |
| 1828 | 56 . . . . . . . . . ./ 25 (including brass & percussion) |

*Milan*
| 1818 | 24 . . . , 6, 6, 7/ 2,2,2,2 (opera) |
|---|---|

[a]Instruments are given in the order violin 1, violin 2, viola, cello, bass/flute, oboe, clarinet, bassoon. Details of brass and percussion are not given, though most orchestras included these instruments. Unless otherwise stated, the orchestra was formed for public concerts.

tos he, too, conducted from the keyboard, filling in as continuo during the tuttis. Recent recordings show how attractive a discreet fortepiano continuo can be.[3]

The orchestral string group probably sounded much as it had done in Handel's time. The structure of the violin itself changed but little during the eighteenth century. Most orchestral instruments would still have had comparatively short necks and light bass bars and sound posts. The strings, moreover, would all have been gut, as indeed they would have been as late as 1900! The resultant sound would still have been much lighter and more articulated than the one that we are now accustomed to (see above, p. 24).

This is not to ignore the fact that substantial changes in instrumental design and playing technique were afoot during Haydn's lifetime.[4] The most important of these changes was undoubtedly the redesign of the bow, which in turn affected the way it was used. The absence of a standard pattern of bow in the early eighteenth century has already been remarked, though a convex stick was a common feature. Surviving mid to late eighteenth-century bows tend to underline the fact that makers and players were searching for a fuller and more sustained sound. François Tourte (1747–1835) eventually came up with the answer in the late 1770s – the concave bow, a design that no subsequent maker has managed to improve. Tourte's later bows are, in fact, indistinguishable from modern ones. The concave curve of the stick permits greater tension on the hair; the tension is adjustable by a screw nut; the bow is heavier than most earlier designs; its point of balance is nearer the nut; and the ribbon of bowing hair is both broader and thicker. The bow made possible a whole new repertory of bow strokes. Without it, for instance, Paganini's wizardry would have been far less spectacular. Tourte's design can hardly have had an immediate impact on orchestral sound, however. The new bow and new ways of using it only gradually infiltrated the orchestral string group as the older players retired, a point that emerges clearly in the following review of April 1810 from *Le Mercure* (Paris):

> Many concerts do not reach the standard of those given at the *Conservatoire*, which are modestly entitled 'student exercises'. The perfection of the performances there surpasses that which distinguished the Concerts Clery. Everyone agrees that this is so, yet nobody knows why. It is important to understand that the string players of the Clery orchestra were pupils of a variety of very good teachers. Each teacher had a different method of bowing. Some used Jarnovic's method, some Tartini's, and a few used Viotti's. This led to a variety of ways of putting the bow to the string and inevitably to a lack of polish and ensemble in performance. Today, three string teachers at the *Conservatoire* – Mssrs Rhode, Kreutzer and Baillot – all base their methods on those of Viotti. The pupils of the three classes all have a broad, energetic manner of playing, one that is so unified that, at a distance, it seems that only one violin is playing.

It would be interesting to know just how far Viotti managed to impose a common bowing discipline upon the members of Haydn's London orchestra! (See especially p. 124 above for a discussion of bowing principles.)

## EIGHTEENTH-CENTURY WIND AND BRASS INSTRUMENTS

Whereas the members of the modern violin family are recognisably the same as their baroque ancestors, modern wind and brass instruments differ considerably from their predecessors.[5] During the first half of the nineteenth century, makers transformed traditional designs, developing elaborate key and valve mechanisms to increase power, simplify fingerings, extend ranges and iron out tonal unevennesses. Baroque flutes, oboes and bassoons are comparatively simple instruments. Up to the time of Mozart the flute commonly had only one key, and even in Beethoven's day it rarely had more than four. The two-keyed oboe that Beethoven knew was still recognisably the instrument that Bach would have known. Eighteenth-century wind instruments are basically diatonic, chromatic notes being produced by cross-fingerings. These cross-fingerings have a quality all their own – writers have described the sounds as veiled, in comparison with open notes. Perceptive composers exploited the expressive potential of veiled notes, and no concern was expressed by any writer of the period at the differences between open and closed notes. Before valves were added to trumpets and horns in the early nineteenth century, only the notes of the harmonic series were generally available, though skilled horn players could obtain chromatic notes by stopping the bell with the left hand. These stopped notes have a particularly veiled and expressive quality. Mozart's use of them in his concertos is particularly noteworthy, as anyone will testify who has heard a good 'authentic' performance on a period instrument.

Generally speaking, then, period instruments are characterised by a greater colour range. Modern instruments iron out tonal inequalities and with them a potentially expressive element in performance. To be sure, eighteenth-century orchestral parts (as opposed to concerto and ensemble parts) tend to avoid the more difficult (and thus, veiled) notes. The horn and trumpet parts of the 'Drum Roll' Symphony, for instance, use only the notes of the harmonic series, whilst the oboe part in the lyrical second subject is considerably simplified in the development section, where the key is – rather awkwardly – D flat [cf. bars 80 and 180 compared with 145].

In terms of actual sound quality, the 'period' flute, horn and trumpet present no difficulties: these can be played with the assurance that they will sound very much as they sounded when they were made. Reed instruments, however, cannot be played without reeds, but few period reeds have survived, and none are in playing condition. Despite the existence of published accounts of reed making, no written description can possibly substitute for the real thing. The tone of an early reed instrument can be transformed by a change of reed – practically anything is possible, from smooth refinement to strident brashness. To judge from Mozart's evident joy at the chance to employ doubled woodwind, however, the chances are that a smooth blend would have been the general ideal toward which orchestral players worked.

Sir Thomas Beecham once advised a colleague not to look at the brass – 'it only encourages them', he observed. The advice is particularly apt as far as the classical symphonic repertory is concerned, for modern brass instruments and modern playing techniques can produce considerably more volume than was possible in Haydn's day. The musical function of the brass group in classical scoring is almost entirely harmonic. Great care needs to be taken therefore, especially in loud tuttis, that the brass – especially the trumpets – do not stand out from the total texture. Modern timpani, too, are liable to swamp the tutti, for eighteenth-century instruments give a much shallower and more brittle sound. A comparison of almost any standard recording of the 'Drum Roll' Symphony, dating from the 1960s or early 1970s, with a good 'authentic' recording made in the 1980s[6] will underline how difficult it is to integrate modern brass and percussion instruments into the orchestral ensemble.

### Tonguing

A good deal can be learned about phrasing and articulation from a study of baroque bowing (see above, p. 24). Tonguing and breathing are the wind equivalents of bowing, and they are equally instructive. In wind music, unslurred notes are articulated by tonguing, which, as Quantz puts it, 'animates the expression of the passions'. The process of tonguing involves the release of pent-up air, the tongue being suddenly relaxed from its closed position against the upper palate or teeth. As we have already seen (p. 14 above), three basic levels of articulation were described, the outer extremes being legato and staccato, the 'normal' articulation lying somewhere in between. The wind player employed four main tonguing consonants to articulate the notes: 'ti', 'di', 'ri' and 'dll' (see Example 118).

ti ti ti ti        ti ti ri ti ri ti        ti di ri di ri di        di dll di dll di dll

**Ex. 118**    Wind instrument tonguing

Every unslurred note had to be articulated by one of these consonants. The choice of consonant depended on the following considerations: how fast the music was going, how vigorous it was and where in the bar the particular note was placed in relation to the main beat. 'Ti' was suitable for 'short, equal, lively and quick notes'; thus successions of equal quavers in 4/4 time could all be tongued 'ti'. This basic single tonguing in which every note was started off with the same syllable, could result, however, in an undesirably explosive effect. It was, moreover, very difficult to do in fast moving passages. For this reason 'ti' was often mixed with 'ri'. 'Ti' would invariably be used for the first note or two of a phrase; it could then be alternated with 'ri' or, if a gentler effect was sought, 'di' could be substituted for 'ti'; 'ri' was placed on the relatively 'good' notes of paired tonguings. 'Ri' is thus directly analogous to the downbow principle of string playing. Where extra fast articulation was required 'di–dll' was used, a combination of consonants that was observed to produce a slight unevenness, 'di' being fractionally longer than 'dll'. The choice of tonguing consonant was of course left to the good taste of the player. When notes were slurred, only the first note of the group was tongued, just as a string player took only one bow for a slurred group. Jacques Hotteterre, in his *Principes de la flûte traversière, ou flûte d'Alle-magne* (Paris, 1707),[7] was the first to point out that flute tonguing produces a much gentler effect than recorder tonguing, and that oboe tonguing is the sharpest of all. On the question of breathing, Quantz is easily the most informative of the many preclassical authors. If a phrase is too long to be taken in one breath, he recommended that breath should be taken wherever possible on tied notes. If the phrase in question includes no such figure but consists of continuous semiquavers (the Allemande of Bach's A minor Partita for unaccompanied flute is a case in point), then breath should be taken between disjunct notes. In the passage given in Example 119, for instance, the player could choose any of the marked points at which to breathe, the breath being taken after the marked note:

**Ex. 119**    Quantz on breathing

Classical composers normally demanded much less of players in the way of breathing, and problems of this kind rarely arise in orchestral parts.

*Tuning*

Early wind instruments were once thought to have had incurable tuning problems. Now that early playing techniques have been rediscovered, this has proved to be an old wives' tale. Indeed, researches have recently shown that the best eighteenth-century wind players were particularly sensitive to the subtleties of intonation, just as singers were. The table in Example 120, edited from Quantz, shows that good players were keenly aware of the difference between such notes as A sharp and B flat, D sharp and E flat, as indeed were singers (see above, p. 84). The numbers represent the holes to be stopped.

*Pitch*

By the second half of the eighteenth century, wind instrument makers were supplying as many as seven different tuning joints (*corps de rechange*) for their

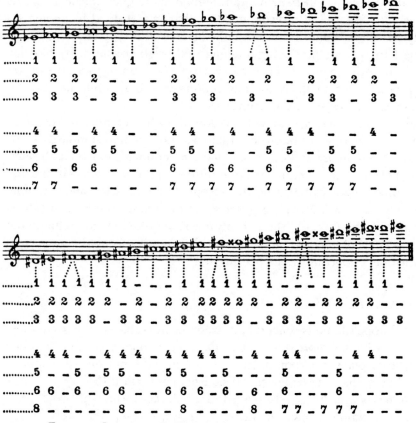

**Ex. 120**   Quantz on wind intonation

instruments, to ensure that players would be able to play at any local pitch that they might encounter. Although pitch varied considerably from place to place, it is clear that both Handel and Bach were working to a standard that lay about a semitone below the modern A = 440: Bach's B minor Mass, in other words, should now be heard in B flat minor and Handel's *Messiah* in D flat. The Viennese maker Stein, whose pianos Mozart so much admired, seems also to have been working to a similar standard in the 1780s. By 1820, the Philharmonic Society in London, which gave the first performance of Beethoven's Ninth Symphony, had adopted a pitch of A = 433; thirty years later 'mean Philharmonic pitch' had reached A = 453. Pitch was also rising at the Paris Opera; indeed, this was a constant source of friction between the singers and the orchestra. By 1880 Broadwood, Erard and Steinway were all tuning to A = 455, and it was only in 1955 that the International Organisation for Standards proposed A = 440, the frequency that is now generally accepted.[8]

Inconvenient as the variable pitch standard must have been, wind players soon learned how to put their many tuning joints to good musical use. As early as 1752 Quantz was recommending that in fast, loud movements a slightly flat joint should be used. The player would correct the pitch by blowing harder, thus producing a louder and brighter sound. By blowing softly, on the other hand, and using a sharp-pitched tuning joint, the player could produce a particularly soft and sombre tone that would be ideal for slow movements, especially in concertos.

On the question of temperament, it is doubtful whether much of use can be said, save for the obvious point that there was no common standard. To be sure, there were many advocates of equal temperament, in which all semitones are of equal size, yet it was not until the mid nineteenth century that equal temperament came to be the accepted standard for piano tuning. Meanwhile, as F. W. Marpurg observed in his *Versuch über die musikalische Temperatur* (Breslau, 1776), 'there is only one kind of equal temperament, but countless kinds of unequal temperament that afford speculative musicians inexhaustible opportunities for variation.'

## CONCERT HALLS

Most of Europe's famous concert halls were considerably smaller than those of today, few having more than 3,000 square feet of floor area. The Salomon concerts took place in a room measuring 79′ by 32′ – one only fractionally larger, that is, than the Holywell Music Room at Oxford (65′ by 32′). The Paris Concerts Spirituels were played in a hall measuring 59′ by 52′. The Leipzig Gewandhaus, newly opened in 1781, was no more than 106′ by 40′. There is some evidence to suggest that audiences may have been crammed in quite tightly, especially for major events. There were normally seats for 800 at the Salomon concerts (the Holywell Music Room now seats about 300), but for Haydn's last benefit concert in May 1795, no fewer than 1,500 people were present. The effect of this on the acoustics may readily be imagined!

## EDITIONS: TWO 'URTEXT' OPTIONS

Two 'Urtext' editions of the Haydn symphonies are currently available: the first by Henle (edited by Hubert Unverricht, hereafter referred to as *HU*), the second by Universal (edited by Robbins Landon: *RL*). They are as different from each other as chalk and cheese. They highlight, in fact, differences in editorial philosophy that have for some years been the subject of heated debate and which need to be understood if the reader is properly to use either edition. Full editorial commentaries are available for both: the *HU* commentary comes separately from the music, however, and is thus less likely to be read than *RL*'s, which is printed at the end of each volume.

Editorial decisions are needed on the following questions: the priority to be accorded to the various kinds of primary source (autograph sketches, autograph composing scores, autograph fair copies, autograph orchestral parts, secondary copies of orchestral parts corrected by the composer, scores/parts published during the composer's lifetime, autograph arrangements) and the importance (if any) of secondary material.

The use that the editor is able to make of these various kinds of source material will depend on such matters as the quality of the composer's handwriting, the relationship between autograph score and orchestral parts (where these are available), the degree of consistency to be observed in the composer's notation, and the relationship between composer and publisher. The quality of the modern edition will above all depend on the attitude that the editor takes to the idea of the *Fassung letzter Hand* – whether, that is, he believes that the latest primary source normally represents the composer's final and *best* thoughts.[9]

The perceived function of the edition will also determine the published format. The editor may set out to produce (a) a diplomatic transcription that attempts to represent as closely as possible the appearance of the original, leaving the reader to resolve all the errors and ambiguities; (b) an edited form of the original, in which ambiguities of notation are interpreted and errors corrected, but no additions are made; or (c) a performing edition in which the editor collates information from all the types of source that he regards as relevant, interpreting ambiguous information, and adding information (especially dynamics, slurs and articulation marks) which he believes has been left out of the original, either through accident or convention.

The two editions of the 'Drum Roll' Symphony may serve to illustrate the debate: *RL* represents category (c); *HU* more or less represents category (b). To understand the nature of the two editions a word must first be said about the primary and secondary sources of the symphony. The primary sources are two: an autograph fair copy score and orchestral parts in the Donaueschingen archives. Although the parts are not autograph they contain copious corrections by Haydn, and they may well represent the London readings of the symphony. Significant secondary material includes a set of parts in the Esterház library which, according to *RL*, are the final texts, and therefore do not contain any corrections by Haydn. There are also two arrangements of the symphony made by Salomon and published by him: one is for piano trio, the other for quintet. Haydn possessed a copy of the trio version. Most importantly there are orchestral parts, published by Robert Birchall (London, c. 1800), which, according to *RL*, 'undoubtedly go back to Salomon's original performance material'.

As *RL* more readily accepts the concept of the *Fassung letzter Hand*, he is more inclined to adjust the text of the autograph score, using the evidence of performance materials which are probably of later date than the score itself.

He gives particular weight to the Birchall printed parts, even though there is no *proof* that Haydn ever saw them or that they do accurately reflect the Salomon parts. The attraction of these parts, and indeed of the Donaues-chingen and Esterház parts is that all provide rather more slurrings and articulation markings than does the autograph score.

Unfortunately, the parts do not merely supplement the score; in places they provide *alternative* readings, by no means all of which are obviously superior to those of the score. Whether such readings should be accepted depends on the perceived relationship of the secondary materials to the autograph fair copy. It could be argued that, as none of the post-score material is actually in Haydn's hand, it cannot be trusted. Haydn was certainly an indifferent proof reader; proofs which he is known to have read still contain numerous errors. *RL*'s great strength is that he fully explains in the edition itself all the amendments he has made to Haydn's score. This is perfectly satisfactory, as long as the user takes the trouble to read the editorial commentary. The actual music notation, however, carries no warning of editorial intrusion. *HU* starts from the assumption that the autograph fair copy is the final authority. The user, therefore, at least knows that *HU*'s edition represents a single integral, primary source.

Two practical examples from the first movement, given as Example 121, may serve to show the characteristics of the two editions:

Ex. 121    Articulation in Haydn's 'Drum Roll' Symphony: the Robbins Landon
edition

The first appearance of the first violin's figure in bar 85 is articulated in all
the major sources.[10] Nowhere else does the autograph score articulate this
figure, apart from the first violin part in bar 222. At this point, however,
Birchall articulates all the moving lines. *RL* adopts Birchall's reading and
notes that he has done so in his commentary. *HU* tidies up the score by
adding editorial articulation in bars 222 (violins 1 and 2) and 224 (violin 2),
making the tidying process visible on the printed page.[11]

These variants raise an important fundamental issue. There has in the
past been an editorial tendency to regularise articulation, insufficient attention being given to the possibility that variation of articulation might be part
of the developmental process. Compare, for instance, bars 47–50 with 125–6
(Example 122).

The second passage is unmarked in the score, but *RL* has added markings
of his own 'on the basis of 47ff', rejecting the Birchall slurring, which begins
on the second note of the bar, not the first. At this point, the whole question of
articulation is wide open, and it should be seen to be so. There is also the

**Ex. 122**   Articulation in Haydn's 'Drum Roll' Symphony: the Robbins Landon
edition

even more crucial matter of the articulation of the first subject, shown in
Example 123. *RL* slurs the semiquaver figures (violin 1, bars 42 and 44 and
their recapitulation equivalents) on the grounds that Haydn supplies this
slurring in bars 105–6 of the autograph score. But retrospective analogies
are surely to be distrusted? Cause for distrust is particularly strong here since
the model slurrings are taken from the development. To what extent, then,
ought the editor to tidy up the original, and to what extent ought the players
to be left to do this for themselves? Opinions seem increasingly to be shifting toward leaving the decisions to the performers, for, although editorial
material may be in round brackets, once it is on the page it will probably be
used.

**Ex. 123**   Articulation in Haydn's 'Drum Roll' Symphony

Hair splitting though the individual problems may seem, cumulatively
they present a considerable interpretative challenge to the performer. As
Webster has observed:

> Those who attempt to recreate eighteenth-century performance practice must
> not remain satisfied with half measures ... They must learn to perform from

eighteenth century musical texts, with all that implies about coming to terms with ambiguity and uncertainty. My colleagues encourage me to hope that someday it will be realised. After all they add articulation to Haydn's autographs as easily as any eighteenth-century scribe, and with greater musical intelligence than many editors. As one of them recently remarked, 'It is a pleasure to have editions that are not cluttered up with someone else's interpretation, so that I can clutter them up with my own.' This is precisely the right attitude. For a scholar or performer to take the additions and adjustments found in a modern edition, *Urtext* or no, as prescriptive or inviolable (as they might be in Schoenberg or even Brahms) would be a falsification of the spirit of Haydn's music.

## A CONTEMPORARY ANALYSIS

The kind of impact that such a work as Haydn's 'Drum Roll' Symphony would have made on an informed audience is suggested, once again, by the French writer Momigny.[12] As before, the discussion is partly programmatic, partly analytical. It opens with a lengthy quotation from Lacépède's *Poétique de la musique*, expressing the postbaroque concept of structure as mood contrast:

> Let us begin with that most remarkable and imposing kind of instrumental music [Lacépède writes]: the symphony. In it, great richness and variety can unite to form a beautiful whole. Pleasurable and moving detail, gentle and enchanting melody may be combined with extended and powerful passages of rapidly moving harmony ... It is a form that is cultivated in the palaces of kings.

To illustrate the concept of contrast, Momigny develops a simple 'pictorial and poetic analysis' for the first movement of the symphony:

1. *Introduction*
   The scene is set in the country. Villagers, alarmed by a raging storm which has been going on since they gathered in church, pray together for deliverance (Momigny refers to the ominous drum rolls, and to the plainsong-like character of the unison opening).
2. *Allegro con Spirito: first section*
   The storm past, they leave the church, the bolder spirits teasing the timorous ones for their recent fears; they express their collective joy at deliverance (bar 48); shepherds and their consorts dance (80); there are renewed expressions of universal joy, and everyone dances (87).
3. *Allegro con Spirito: second section* [viz. development]
   Further taunting exchanges between the bold and the timid (note the mocking appearance of the speeded-up introduction at 112) are followed by a second dance (144), which rises to a tumultuous climax.

4. *Allegro con Spirito: third section* [viz. recapitulation]

This mirrors the opening of section one (the exposition); at bar 189, however, a heated argument breaks out; violent passions are roused, and all is about to disintegrate. The recurrence of the thunder (202) brings everyone to their senses. After further prayers the storm clouds disperse and the movement ends in renewed joy.

Momigny's technical analysis is much less detailed than the one that he supplies for Mozart's D minor Quartet, especially in respect of key (see above, p. 113). This analysis focuses particularly on the idea of variety within unity, and on Haydn's skill in avoiding the obvious. Momigny admires the varied symmetry of the 'Intrada' (one-bar drum roll, then 6+6, 6+6 and 14). He appreciates Haydn's clever avoidance of obvious perfect cadences – notably at the end of the 'Intrada', at bars 71, 86–7, 113–4 and 150; and he draws attention to the ways in which the *périodes* set each other off, by motivic, textural and dynamic contrasts. He even sees the fifth period [i.e. the second group] as a lyrical (and typical) contrast to the *premier sujet* (bars 40–7).

*A Summary of Momigny's analysis*

*Intrada*

| | |
|---|---|
| Three periods: 1–13, 14–25, 25/2–39 | note the exquisitely varied scoring for wind and horns, especially the 'magical' B flats for horns, 19–20 |

*Allegro con spirito* [Exposition]
Period

| | | |
|---|---|---|
| 1 | [first group] | 40–7 opening *pp* [sic] to heighten the impact of 2 |
| 2 | [transition/1] | 48–59 *période de verve*, *f*, full of warmth and vivacity |
| 3 | [transition/2] | 60–3 a 'mixed' period of *p* and *f* |
| 4 | [transition/3] | 64–79 *f*, rising to a shattering *ff*; b. 71 a 'masterstroke' |
| 5 | [second group] | 80–6 *période mélodieuse* with simple Italianate accompaniment |
| 6 | [codetta] | 87–94 *lieu commun* – a kind of refrain or *Gloria patri*: yet Haydn gives individuality to it: the material is not 'banal', but develops from the preceding *période* |

*Second Section of the Movement* [Development]

| | | |
|---|---|---|
| 1 | [from first group] | 94–104 contrapuntal textures provide new interest after the 'fracas' of the codetta |
| 2 | [from first group] | 105–12 increased contrapuntal complexity, further heightens the interest |

| | | | |
|---|---|---|---|
| 3 | [from Intrada] | 112–19/2 | speeded up, with a commentary from the first and second violins |
| 4 | [from transition/1] | 119–129 | a conversation develops between first and second violins |
| 5 | [from first group] | 130–143 | further truncation of the *sujet*: cf 94– |
| 6 | [from second group] | 144–9 | an unexpected twist, since a return of the *premier sujet*, b. 40, had been prepared |
| 7 | [from second group] | 150–9 | a further skilful postponement of the tonic cadence |

*Third Section of the Movement* [Recapitulation]

| | | | |
|---|---|---|---|
| 1 | [first group] | 159–166 | note for note as [exposition] |
| 2 | [transition/1] | 167–179 | suitably shortened |
| 3 | [second group] | 180–6 | compare scoring with bars 80 and 130 |
| 4 | [second group (development)] | 187–201 | compare the heightened impact of 184–201 with 66–80 |

*Intrada*

| | | | |
|---|---|---|---|
| 5 | [cf. Development 3] | 214–20 | |
| 6 | [Coda] | 220–9 | [as exposition codetta] |

# 11

## Beethoven's 'Moonlight' Sonata and late eighteenth-century pianism

### CLAVICHORD, HARPSICHORD AND EARLY PIANO

Although the piano was invented at the beginning of the eighteenth century, it made little headway against established keyboard instruments before 1750. As we have seen, J. S. Bach was unimpressed by the piano (p. 12 above), though he appears to have changed his mind after trying out Silbermann's latest instruments at Dresden in 1747. Even so, German-speaking musicians continued to use the expressive clavichord for many years after, whilst in England, France, Spain and Italy the harpsichord long remained a popular instrument. Some idea of the slow progress that the piano at first made is illustrated in the list of events in Table 6.[1]

Table 6. From clavichord and harpsichord to piano: some significant dates

1763: Vienna – the first appearance of a piano in a public concert
1763: Leopold Mozart purchases a Stein clavichord for Wolfgang to use as a practice instrument on their travels
1767: Dibdin plays 'a new instrument called the pianoforte' in London
1768: The piano is first played at the Paris *Concerts Spirituels*. The pianist is J. C. Bach
1770: Leopold Mozart buys a harpsichord
1772: The first English 'grand' pianos are made in London by Backers: his assistants are Broadwood and Stodart
1773: Stein develops an escapement for the Viennese piano
1778: Erard begins making square pianos in Paris
1779: Mozart's employer, the Archbishop of Salzburg, buys a square piano
1779: Clementi plays concertos in London, the first on harpsichord, the second on piano
1785: Twelve pianists play at the Paris *Concerts Spirituels* during the season, as against one harpsichordist
1791: Haydn directs performances of his symphonies at the London 'Salomon' concerts, from the fortepiano
1793: Shudi and Broadwood cease making harpsichords
1796: Erard begins making English action grand pianos in Paris
1799: The Paris *Conservatoire* awards an annual prize for piano playing, and discontinues the harpsichord prize

Broadly speaking, there were two eighteenth-century schools of piano making: one was Viennese, the other was English and French. The two types of piano were very different in structure and in sound. The Viennese was more akin to the clavichord; its key action was light and shallow, and its resonance was thin and bright, the transparent tone being made all the clearer by a very efficient damping mechanism. The so-called 'English-action' piano was the direct descendant of Cristofori's original fortepiano. Its complicated escapement action threw the hammer faster against the string than did the Viennese action. Because of this, and because the English piano tended to have larger hammers, the instrument could in theory at least produce a louder *forte* than the Viennese piano. It lacked the clarity and brightness of the Viennese sound, however, and perhaps for this reason was found to be less effective as a concerto instrument. The lack of clarity was in part due to the English damping system, which was less efficient than the Viennese one; English action dampers merely rested on top of the strings, the upper notes being wholly undamped. The English must have preferred the slightly blurred effect that the damping produced, for they could easily have produced an efficient damping system had they so wished.

The Viennese piano was the one that Haydn and Mozart preferred. The English piano was the one best known to Clementi, who was seen by Czerny as the founder of a school of 'soft, quiet and melodious' pianism, a school that was developed by Dussek and Cramer. From all that has been said about the differing qualities of Viennese and English pianos, Beethoven might well have been expected to prefer the English instrument, for it was particularly well suited to music of a singing, legato character. As is well known, moreover, the French Erard firm presented him with an English action piano in 1803, whilst the firm of Broadwood gave him a six-octave CC–C$^4$ grand piano in 1818. Yet Beethoven found both instruments cumbersome and unsatisfactory to play, and, in spite of increasing deafness, he remained faithful to the lighter Viennese design.[2] Both styles of instrument were being constantly 'improved'; it is therefore impossible to identify a specifically *Mozart* or *Beethoven* piano. To be sure, Beethoven remained in close touch with the Steins and Streichers in Vienna. No instruments by either family can definitely be associated with him, however, since (as Newman suggests) the makers were probably only too happy to lend him their latest designs and to change them as they were superseded.

## KEYBOARD INSTRUCTION BOOKS

The most influential keyboard tutor of the eighteenth century was undoubtedly C. P. E. Bach's *Essay on the True Art of Playing Keyboard Instruments*. Haydn, Mozart and Beethoven all used it, as did Beethoven's young pupil Carl Czerny – piano virtuoso, composer and author of one of the most important nineteenth-century books on piano playing. The keyboard instruments that C. P. E. Bach discusses in his book are the clavichord (his favourite), the harpsichord, the organ and the fortepiano. Like most eighteenth-century teachers, Bach taught the same basic technique for all four types of keyboard instrument. It is one that is ideally suited to the clavichord, a delicate instrument calling for the most sensitive finger control. When playing the clavichord there is no question of using arm weight or wrist action, as a heavy and energetic touch will ruin the tuning. German writers were still making the point, as late as 1791, that the clavichord was the ideal instrument for young beginners, since it encouraged the development of a quietly controlled finger action.

The first keyboard tutor to address itself primarily to the pianist was J. P. Milchmeyer's *Die wahre Art das Pianoforte zu spielen* (Dresden, 1797). Other piano tutors and books of studies soon followed – notably Muzio Clementi's *Introduction to the Art of Playing on the Piano Forte* (London, 1801), and Louis Adam's *Méthode de Piano* (Paris, 1804), which was adopted by the Paris *Conservatoire*. As far as basic hand positioning and finger action were concerned, there was nothing revolutionary in any of these piano methods; indeed, the piano virtuoso and pedagogue Johann Nepomuk Hummel was still teaching a technique in the 1820s that was recognisably the same as that described by C. P. E. Bach.[3]

Early pianos can easily be made to jangle if the keys are depressed too forcefully. The comments of the Viennese piano maker and teacher Johann Andreas Streicher suggest that many people were insensitive to this fact:

> If the tone of the pianoforte is to move and please the listener it should as much as possible resemble the sound of the best wind instruments . . . In a *fortissimo* [the good pianist] makes us believe that we are listening to an organ or to the fulness of an orchestra, by lifting the dampers . . . He knows how to let every note *sing* without straining his instrument . . . Why [Streicher asks] does the pianist force the tone more than any other instrumentalist?[4]

If the hands are properly held, and if touch is basically a matter of finger action, there will be no danger of jangling sounds and forced tone.

### Fingerings

It is unfortunate that neither Haydn nor Mozart has left us any keyboard fingerings.[5] As both composers were familiar with C. P. E. Bach's *Versuch*, however, we may safely assume that they fingered their music very much as Bach would have done. Although Bach did not completely discard the paired fingerings of earlier systems, he used thumbs and little fingers extensively, and he developed 'thumbs under' fingerings for scales in the modern manner.[6]

Of all the classical and early romantic composers, Beethoven is the only one to have specified fingerings at all extensively. Just over three hundred markings are to be found in his autographs, sketches and first editions. The importance that he attached to properly thought-out fingerings is evident from his correspondence in 1817 with Czerny, who was then teaching his nephew Carl the piano. Under no circumstances, Beethoven wrote, was Czerny to discuss matters of interpretation with the boy until fingerings, notes and rhythms were completely mastered.

Two pieces in particular illustrate the basic principles of fingering that Beethoven taught his piano pupils, principles that were founded on C. P. E. Bach's *Versuch* – a book that he used, incidentally, when he taught Czerny. The pieces are the Sonatine in F WoO 50/1, which he composed for Franz Wegeler about 1790, and a one-movement Trio in B flat WoO 39 headed 'Vienna, 26 June, 1812, for my little friend Maxe Brentano to encourage her in piano playing . . . L.v.Bthvn.' Two passages from the piano part of the Trio (Example 124) illustrate the essential points of Beethoven's fingering.

**Ex. 124**   Beethoven's fingering in the Trio WoO39

*Early styles of pianism and the development of the legato touch*

While the sounds of early pianos and the techniques of early pianists can be recreated with some confidence, it is less easy to know for sure just how the great early pianists would actually have played – particularly Mozart and Beethoven. Mozart declared that he taught his pupils a 'quiet, even touch', in which the qualities of 'natural lightness' and 'smooth rapidity' were essential ingredients. Beethoven saw Mozart's own playing in quite a different light, as his pupil Czerny tells us:

> Beethoven told me [he wrote] that he had heard Mozart play on several occasions and that Mozart, since at that time the invention of the piano was still in its infancy, had accustomed himself to a manner of playing . . . then more frequently used, which was in no way adapted to the fortepiano. In course of time I also made the acquaintance of several persons who had taken lessons from Mozart, and found this remark justified by their playing . . . even after Mozart's day, the choppy, short, detached manner of playing was the fashion.[7]

Undoubtedly Czerny's comments are not solely to do with performance style. They bear upon the kind of music that Mozart wrote, and on the quality of sound produced by the early Viennese piano. Yet Mozart's technique does seem to have been a more highly articulated one than Beethoven's, even though Mozart had as his ideal a singing style of performance.

The anglicised Clementi may well have been the first influential performer to develop a truly pianistic style.[8] In his *Introduction to the Art of Playing on the Piano Forte*, Clementi declared that it was best 'to adhere chiefly to the legato, reserving the staccato to give spirit occasionally to certain passages, and to set off the higher beauties of the legato' (p. 9). One of his pupils, Louis Berger, later asked him whether he had always followed this advice. He freely admitted that he used to play quite differently but that subsequently he had achieved 'a more melodic and noble style of performance after listening attentively to famous singers'. He also attributed the change in part to the development of the English piano, 'the construction of which formerly stood in the way of a cantabile and legato style of playing'.

Attention has recently been focused especially on the change that occurred during the late eighteenth century in the concept of a 'normal' legato. Up to the time of Daniel Türk the normal allegro legato had been achieved by releasing one note somewhat before the next was played, in the manner described by C. P. E. Bach and Quantz (see above, p. 16). From the early years of the nineteenth century, however, Clementi's legato touch became the norm, each note being held its full length.[9]

## Pedalling

An important aspect of the growing concern for a pianistic legato was the development of the art of managing the sustaining pedal.[10] At first, pedals were regarded by serious musicians with suspicion, since these included such gimmicky effects as 'Turkish music', 'bassoons' and the like. On the earliest pianos, stops (not pedals) were used to lift the dampers from the strings. At first, therefore, the sustaining mechanism was a comparatively inflexible device. By 1777 Mozart was praising the piano maker Stein for a new invention that allowed the dampers to be operated by knee levers, just six years before the English maker John Broadwood patented a foot pedal for actuating them. Even so, there is much evidence to show that Mozart used the pedals somewhat sparingly, and at times not at all. In the 1780s he added an organ-style pedalboard to a grand piano of his, regardless of the fact that it must greatly have hampered control of the 'soft' and 'sustaining' knee levers; he may have used this pedal clavier to give greater weight to the bottom line in performances of his D minor Concerto (K466).

Whilst the use of the sustaining pedal increased rapidly from 1800 onwards, Hummel could still write in 1828 that a truly great artist had 'no occasion for pedals to work upon his audience by expression and power', even though the 'damper' and 'piano' pedals were capable of 'agreeable effects'. Surprisingly perhaps, Schubert greatly admired Hummel's playing, to the extent that he had intended to dedicate to him his three great piano sonatas, D958, 959 and 960. Czerny observed, incidentally, that those who admired Hummel's playing thought that Beethoven created 'nothing but confused noise in the use of the pedal'. As late as 1830 the virtuoso pianist and teacher Christian Kalkbrenner was urging the Germans to take the sustaining pedal seriously. Without it, he declared, they would never achieve 'that beautiful manner of *singing*' which so distinguishes the playing of the English school.[11]

The first published instructions on the use of the damper and *una corda* pedals are to be found in Louis Adam's *Méthode* of 1804. Oddly enough, Clementi said nothing about the subject until the fifth (1811) edition of his piano method, even though the foremost pianists of the English school – Franz Dussek (1760–1812), Johann Baptist Cramer (1771–1858) and John Field (1782–1837) – had been using the pedals extensively well before then, as indeed had Beethoven.

The earliest printed pedal markings are in Clementi's Op. 37 Sonatas of 1798, though the marks suggest that the composer had stops in mind rather than pedals. Only in the Op. 40 Sonatas of 1802 are the pedallings complicated enough to suggest that they were intended for the feet. Certainly Mozart had not considered pedalling important enough to notate it in his music. The same is true of Haydn, save for an occasional 'open' pedal direction, as in bar 73 of the Allegro of the Piano Sonata in C HXVI:50.

Czerny was the first to say much about the shifting (or as we would call it, 'soft') pedal. The point that he made is an important one to grasp, namely that the shifting action produced not only a softer sound, but a different *quality* of sound. He therefore believed that it was to be used with discrimination, and not simply whenever the music was marked *piano*:

> The shifting pedal [he observed] not only renders the tone softer but also gives it a melodious and different character. That player therefore would commit a great fault who should produce the *piano* at every soft passage by means of this pedal. On all good instruments of the present day we can and ought to produce each degree of loud and soft *by touch alone*. The shifting pedal should only be used where we wish still more to enhance the delicacy in beautiful and melodious passages.[12]

## EDITIONS

An essential part of any enquiry into performance style must of course deal with the question of text (see particularly p. 156 above for discussion of editorial principles and problems). The first point to keep in mind is that Beethoven did care a good deal about textual accuracy, and that he expected the performer scrupulously to respect his intentions. His correspondence with publishers makes this amply clear, though, alas, it is equally clear that his publishers often fell short of his expectations.[13] His correspondence suggests, too, that even his close associates sometimes took liberties with his music when they played it. On one occasion he must have lost his temper with Czerny for this. 'You must forgive a composer [he later apologised] who would rather have heard the music played as written, however beautifully you played it in other respects.' No doubt Czerny had this in mind when, in his study *The Art of Playing the Ancient and Modern Pianoforte Works*, he insisted that 'generally in all classical authors the player must by no means allow himself to alter the composition, nor to make any addition or abbreviation'.[14] (According to the unreliable Schindler, Czerny in later life took increasing liberties with Beethoven's music, adding ornaments in the manner of the new school of velocity, and keeping a 'metronome-like regularity of pulse'.)[15] Many of the questions about the physical characteristics of Beethoven's original texts can only be answered of course by the editor, who must be judged by the quality of the commentaries that he appends to his editions. A glance at the sources of the C sharp minor Sonata Op. 27 No. 2 may serve, however, to illustrate the kinds of problem that arise in Beethoven's music. In this particular case we have both the composer's fair copy and the first 'authentic' edition published by Cappi (Vienna, 1802).[16]

Although Beethoven was an impetuously untidy writer, his intentions are generally clear enough; indeed, he notated dynamics and articulation marks rather more fully and consistently than did Haydn and Mozart, although his slurs are no more carefully drawn than theirs. A glance at the first edition of the C sharp minor Sonata shows that the printer must have worked from some other manuscript, possibly a professional copy revised by Beethoven, since there are distinct differences between the autograph and the print. Even so, there are close parallels in, for instance, the ways that the hairpin crescendos and diminuendos are drawn: the peaks of the crescendos between bars 28 and 31, for instance, tend to occur just *after* the third beat, and not (as many later editions suggest) *on* it. Throughout the second movement, the placing of the staccato marks is remarkably similar in the two sources. In the third movement, the left-hand staccato marks are identical, as are the pedallings. The printer was evidently doing his best to reproduce the appearance of the copy that Beethoven sent him.[17] Despite such care, however, the first edition is not error free, the most glaring mistake being in the eleventh bar, where natural signs against the left-hand Ds are lacking, a mistake that Beethoven would surely have picked up!

Clear as most of the notation is in both autograph and print, its interpretation is by no means straightforward. There are extensive phrasings; but what do they mean, especially the somewhat wayward markings of the first movement? How is the first movement instruction 'senza sordino' to be interpreted? What are the speeds that Beethoven had in mind for the three movements? And how flexibly would Beethoven have played each movement? General answers to these questions will be found in many different kinds of source, especially in Czerny's Op. 500 *Complete . . . Pianoforte School* and its supplement, a strangely neglected mine of information on early nineteenth-century performance practice. To be sure, Czerny did not publish his Beethoven chapters (in Op. 500, vol. 4) until 1838, eleven years after Beethoven had died. He did, however, have a phenomenal musical memory (he could play all the piano works by heart) and he had studied quite a few of the sonatas with Beethoven, probably, as Paul Badura-Skoda suggests, including Op. 27 No. 2. His comments must be taken seriously, then, despite all that Schindler says to the contrary.[18]

In the first movement of the 'Moonlight' Sonata there is considerably more cross-bar slurring than is to be found in the piano music of Haydn and Mozart (see Example 125). No fewer than four slurs cover two whole bars each, quite a few others begin on the upbeat to a bar and there are varied patterns of slurring within bars – the opening two bars are unslurred, the third bar is slurred in two groups of six quavers, the fourth in one, the fifth in four groups of three and so on. But Beethoven also asks the player to play the piece with the utmost delicacy and with the dampers off (*Si deve suonare tutto questo pezzo delicatissimamente e senza sordino*). This means that whatever the slurring is, the general effect is a continuous legato. Lest Beethoven's true intention be doubted here, it is worth recalling Czerny's earwitness account of Beethoven's performance of the Op. 37 C minor Piano Concerto in 1803:

**Ex. 125**  Phrasing in the first edition of Beethoven's 'Moonlight' Sonata

Beethoven [he wrote], who publicly played this concerto in 1803, continued the pedal during the entire theme, which on the weak-sounding pianofortes of that day did very well, especially when the shifting pedal was also used (Op. 500, vol. 4, p. 107).

[Czerny was also well aware that things had changed a good deal since then, for he continued:] now as the instruments have acquired a much greater body of tone, we should advise the damper to be employed anew at each important change of harmony, but in such a manner that no cessation of the sound may be observed.

[This was precisely what he advised for the first movement of the 'Moonlight':] the prescribed pedal must be re-employed at each note in the bass [he suggested]; and all must be played *legatissimo*.[19]


What then do the slurs mean? On closer inspection they seem to have two functions. In the first case slurs are placed over the melodic line whenever the notes change pitch – the repeated G sharps of bars 5–6 are unslurred, for instance, whereas the moving line from 7–9 is slurred. Beethoven surely does this to remind the player that, although the sustaining pedal may be 're-employed at each note in the bass',[20] a continuous legato must be maintained. The other type of slur seems to be more in the nature of a phrase mark, controlling the flow of the music rather than the articulation of figuration. On the rising phrases of bars 32–5 the phrasing divides into bar-long units and coincides with the rate of harmonic change; there could well be a slight tenuto at the start of each bar. Bars 36–7, on the other hand, are slurred together as the tessitura moves downward and the tension decreases. The slurring in bars 62–7 similarly suggests a lessening of tension. The origins of late nineteenth-century phrasing can perhaps be traced back to passages such as these.

The articulation of the second movement is unambiguous, save for one or two minor details. Much play is made of the slurred upbeat/downbeat pattern and of staccato accompanying textures, which are consistently indicated by dots. At certain parts of the last movement, however, such as bars 6, 8, 14 and 37, the autograph score shows dashes; at most of these points the first edition shows dots (see Example 126), but, on the other hand, it gives dashes in bars 21, 25 and 65. Czerny makes no distinction between the two in his Op. 500 piano tutor, and it may well be that in the early works Beethoven also intended no difference. It is perhaps significant that the two recent urtext editions of the D major Sonata Op. 10 No. 3 fail to agree as to whether Beethoven wrote dashes or dots in the first movement. As a letter about the Op. 132 A minor Quartet indicates, however,[21] Beethoven was by then distinguishing between them, though he fails, alas, to explain just what the difference should be! Presumably the dashes are more accentual than the dots?

**Ex. 126**   Dotting in Beethoven's 'Moonlight' Sonata

A further and by now familiar point arises in connection with the articulation: how far to extend an established pattern of articulation when none is indicated in the score. Beethoven marks the left-hand figuration in bars 1 and 65 of the last movement staccato. The following bars in each case are unmarked (see above, p. 14). Clearly the staccato must continue until the figuration changes, as, indeed, Czerny confirms:

> The whole [must be] extremely impetuous, and with a powerful, clear and brilliant touch. For the two chords marked 'ff' the pedal must always be used. The quavers in the bass, very staccato ... The second part precisely similar ...

Beethoven used an increasingly complex Italian vocabulary of performance directions in his later works. Before 1812 he used only five ways of indicating soft, expressive playing: *dolce, dolce molto legato, sempre dolce e piano, espressivo* and *molto cantabile.* He subsequently added to these *teneramente, sempre dolce cantabile, cantabile ed espressivo, un poco espressivo, molto espressivo, espressivo e semplice, molto espressivo e semplice, con intimissimo sentimento* and *dolente.* His concern here to capture the mood of the music as closely as possible in words is matched by his lavish use of dynamic markings. He used crescendo and diminuendo (and their equivalent hairpins) far more freely than any predecessor had done. His range of other dynamic markings, too, is far broader, and the distinctions between *pianos* and *fortes* more marked than his predecessors'. The C Sharp minor Sonata, for instance, begins as softly as possible (*pianissimo*); the melody when it enters in the fifth bar is marked *pp*, which, as Czerny points out, 'must be delivered with rather more emphasis'. The last movement is full of dynamic surprises, including two *ff* chords for which, Czerny tells us, 'the pedal must always be used'. Of course, the available dynamic range was much narrower than it is now, and Beethoven might well have revelled in both the sustaining power and dynamic potential of the modern instrument. He would surely have regretted, however, its loss of attack – the sheerly percussive quality that a Viennese piano can impart to such a movement as the C sharp minor.

## TEMPOS

Czerny and Hummel placed the Italian terms for speed in much the same order as earlier writers had done (see above, p. 134), moving from Grave to Presto. There is no reason to suppose that Beethoven would have disagreed with them. He did, however, use the term 'assai' in a way that was peculiar to himself. Several important authorities, including Leopold Mozart and Hummel, interpreted assai as an intensification of the prevailing speed; therefore, when they wrote 'Allegro assai' and 'Adagio assai' the speeds were to be respectively faster and slower than normal. Beethoven, on the other hand, used assai to temper a given speed. The clue to this is found in the song cycle *An die ferne Geliebte* (Op. 98). Towards the end of the second song the Italian 'Allegro assai' is duplicated by the German 'Ziemlich geschwind' (rather fast). The implication here is unmistakable.[22]

Beethoven often seems to be wrestling with the imprecision of words in order to convey precisely the speed that he has in mind. There is, for instance, his exceptionally inventive 'Andante con moto assai vivace quasi allegretto ma non troppo' at the beginning of the C major Mass! Was this a gentle dig, perhaps, at people who took such directions too seriously, or was it the outward sign of inner frustration at the vagueness of words? He certainly gave the warmest welcome to Mr Maelzel's metronome when it first appeared in 1813 as the potential solution to the problem of tempo. Although he subsequently published metronome markings for the symphonies and string quartets (up to and including Opus 95) and for one or two other works, he left the piano sonatas unmarked apart from the 'Hammerklavier' Sonata Op 106.[23] Although Czerny suggested metronome marks in his edition of the piano sonatas,[24] these are not consistent with the markings that he published in his *On the Proper Performance of all Beethoven's Works for Piano*; on the evidence of these markings, Czerny seems to have speeded up his performance of the C sharp minor Sonata by the time he came to edit the complete works. Of the early editors, Liszt took the slowest view of the first movement; Czerny did quite properly draw attention to the alla breve marking, however, and he suggested that the movement ought to be played 'in moderate *Andante* time'.

Table 7. Metronome markings in early
editions and modern performances of the
'Moonlight' Sonata

|  | Mvt. 1 | Mvt. 2 | Mvt. 3 |
|---|---|---|---|
| Czerny/Op. 500 | c 54 | m. 76 | m 80 |
| Simrock/Czerny | c 60 | m. 80 | m 92 |
| Liszt | c 50 | m. 76 | m 84 |
| Gilels | c 46 | m. 63 | m 78 |
| Brendel | c 48 | m. 56 | m 76 |

(c = crotchet, m = minim, m. = dotted minim)

Many of Beethoven's metronome markings seem to be on the fast side.
Recent research, nonetheless, suggests that Beethoven's contemporaries –
and indeed Beethoven himself – took his music at speeds that are very much
in line with those to be heard today.[25]

The English conductor Sir George Smart meticulously annotated London
Philharmonic Society programmes between 1819 and 1843, mainly those of
performances he himself had directed. Timings of works about which there
can be no possible ambiguity – i.e. works that have no repeats or cadenzas –
show that contemporary performances took much the same time as modern
ones; the timings also show that, for London performances of the orchestral
repertory at least, repeats were not normally played.

Table 8. Some early nineteenth-century timings

| Beethoven | | |
|---|---|---|
| *Choral Fantasia* | 20 minutes | 19 minutes[a] |
| Overture: *Fidelio* | 7 | 6 |
| Overture: *Coriolan* | 10 | 8 |
| Overture: *Egmont* | 10 | 8 |
| Ninth Symphony: 1st mvt. | 14 | 15 |
| 3rd mvt. | 12 | 15 |
| 4th mvt. | 23 | 24 |
| Mendelssohn | | |
| Overture: *A Midsummer Night's Dream* | 11 | 11 |

[a] Column 1 gives Smart's timing, column 2 an average of three
recorded performances.

Some movements here are a little faster, some a little slower than the average
times recently recorded by three distinguished conductors. The conclusion
must be, then, that present ideas about nineteenth-century speeds are on the
right lines.

Smart was no provincial figure. He had played in the Salomon concerts
under Haydn. He was very familiar with European traditions. Many members of his Philharmonic orchestra had played in foreign orchestras. He had

himself visited Beethoven in 1825, when the composer had spent a good deal of time, Smart tells us, 'playing the subjects on the piano of many movements of his symphonies'.[26]

## ORNAMENTS: THE EVIDENCE OF HUMMEL AND CZERNY

Both Hummel and Czerny approached ornamentation from a similarly undogmatic standpoint, referring disparagingly to the complexity of earlier and outmoded conventions. To judge from the little concrete evidence that has survived – principally in the form of fingered ornaments – Beethoven, too, seems to have treated ornamentation somewhat freely.

Hummel and Czerny proposed four main categories of ornament: appoggiaturas, mordents, turns and trills. Appoggiaturas were either short or long, and all were played on the beat. The short ones were in the nature of what we now call acciaccaturas, being played as fast as possible, and notated as shown in Example 127.

Ex. 127   Czerny: some acciaccaturas

Long appoggiaturas, 'often employed in the older class of Compositions', were still used from time to time, though Czerny felt that they ought to be written out in normal notation in order to avoid confusion. From his illustrations, given in Example 128, it will be seen that the small note takes half the value of the main note, or two thirds of it when that main note is dotted. Mordents presented no problems, following always on the pattern shown in Example 129, the upper note being in the key of the passage concerned:

Ex. 128    Czerny: some appoggiaturas

Ex. 129    Czerny: some mordents

Czerny listed three types of turn: the simple turn, the double turn and the triple turn (see Example 130), all of which were to be played quickly, 'for a sluggish and dawdling turn produces scarcely any effect'.

Whilst the double turn was normally identified by a single grace note preceding it, Czerny's own transcriptions suggest that he would normally have played a double turn, whether or not there was a grace note preceding it, particularly where the turn sign was placed after the note to which it was to be applied. Czerny also admitted the possibility of a slowish turn at important phrase endings.

Trills were to be played 'with the utmost rapidity and equality'. Unless a long trill went straight into a second one, it would end with a turn, whether or not the turn was actually notated. It could start in one of three ways. When the preceding note was of the same pitch as the principal note the trill would begin on the upper auxiliary. The trill could, however, start on the lower auxiliary when a 'striking effect' was aimed at, and when the trill itself was of 'considerable length'. Normally, however, the trill was to start on the main note. Beethoven, too, allowed the possibility of main-note and upper-

**Ex. 130**   Czerny: some turns

note starts; seven of the twelve trills that he fingered must start on the main note and four on the upper note.[27] Czerny observed that many of his contemporaries used the sign of the 'imperfect shake' when they wished the trill to end without a turn (Example 131).

**Ex. 131**   Czerny: some trills

Oddly enough, although he conceded the possibility of slowing the trill down (Example 132), Czerny made no mention of speeding it up.

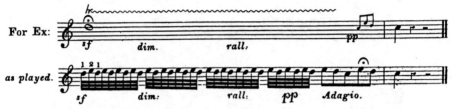

Ex. 132   Czerny: the decelerating trill

Within the section on ornamentation Czerny discussed the rhythmic interpretation of florid melodic lines consisting of 'irregular and unusual numbers of notes which are often difficult to distribute against the accompaniment' (see Example 133). In such cases, the left hand was to provide the regular pulse, the right-hand melody being set freely against it. Czerny warned that any attempt to measure out the melody would inevitably sound 'stiff and ineffective'; the notes should, moreover, be played effortlessly 'without the smallest movement of the hand', the fingers lightly and gently touching the keys to produce articulation midway between staccato and legato.

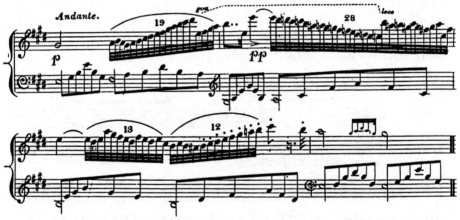

Ex. 133   Czerny: rhythm in melismatic music

Czerny devoted the closing paragraphs of his discussion of ornamentation to arpeggiated chords. He suggested that they could be effective if used sparingly. The speed of the arpeggio could vary from slow to fast, depending on context. In the passage shown in Example 134, for instance, 'the single notes of the arpeggioed [*sic*] chords must follow one another extremely slowly, *and we only begin to count the time prescribed from the last and highest note*' (as for instance at the very opening of the Op. 31 No. 2 Sonata).

**Ex. 134**    Czerny: the arpeggio

## RHYTHMIC FLEXIBILITY

For all that has so far been said about the interpretation of Beethoven's music, one elusive yet vitally important ingredient remains for discussion: the extent to which the rhythmic flow of the music would have been nuanced. Czerny undoubtedly considered this to be one of the most crucial issues:

> We now come to the third and perhaps the most important means of Expression [he wrote], namely to the various changes in the Time first prescribed, by means of the *rallentando* and *accelerando*, or the dragging and hurrying onwards in the degree of movement.
>
> That Time is infinitely divisible . . . we have already remarked. Before everything else we must consider it as a rule, always to play each piece of music from beginning to end, without the least deviation or uncertainty, in the time prescribed by the author, and first fixed upon by the player. But without injury to this maxim there occurs *almost in every line* [my italics] some notes or passages, where a small and often almost imperceptible relaxation or acceleration of the movement is necessary, to embellish the expression and increase the interest.
>
> To introduce these occasional deviations from the strict keeping of the time in a tasteful and intelligible manner, is the great art of a good player; and is only to be acquired by highly cultivated taste, much attentive practice, and by listening to great Artists on all instruments, particularly to distinguished singers.[28]

Czerny's ultimate objective was expressive playing. 'Each single passage [he wrote] expresses some definite passion or emotion; or at least it will admit of some such feeling being infused into it, by the style in which it may be played.' Some 'slight holding back in the time (*calando, smorzando*, etc.) may generally be introduced to advantage' when the music suggests such feelings as 'wavering hesitation, tender complaining, tranquil assent, whispering a secret, sighing, and grief'. Some speeding of the time, on the other hand, will

**Ex. 135**    Four interpretations of Czerny

reinforce feelings of 'sudden cheerfulness, impatience, unwilling reproach, pride, and ill temper'.

Though we may smile at these simple descriptions of musical expression, we have to remind ourselves that Czerny was one of Beethoven's most distinguished and respected pupils, and that he must at least in part have been reflecting his master's teachings in his own writings. Czerny suggested, for instance, that the passage in Example 135 might be played in a number of different ways, ranging from the totally strict (no. 1) to the very free (no. 4). As Czerny felt that the character of the music was 'soft, tender and extremely timid', the first alternative was scarcely possible, no matter how carefully the player handled the dynamics and phrasing. The second was perhaps better, since the ritenuto made more of the crescendo. The third, however, was best, as it gave 'life and warmth' to the first two ascending bars and imparted to the final rallentando a much more 'pleasing effect'. As far as the fourth alternative was concerned, Czerny felt that it was 'too spun out', and that only a very 'delicate mode of touch' could make it at all acceptable. He warned particularly against excesses of rhythmic variation, and hurrying, advising that the ritardando was generally more effective than the accelerando. He suggested a number of different contexts in which the music might be slightly held back: just before a recapitulation, at the introduction of some contrasting theme, during a passage of long and sustained notes which needed emphasising, immediately before a change of speed, immediately after a pause, during a diminuendo after a lively passage, during the course of a highly elaborated melody and in 'humorous, capricious and fantastic' passages, in order to 'heighten the character so much the more'. Rhythmic give and take was also appropriate, Czerny said, when the music was marked 'espressivo'.

Czerny's not uninteresting and somewhat Schubertian Andantino (Example 136) gives a good idea of the extent to which his advice might be applied to an extended piece of music.

**Ex. 136**   Czerny's Andantino espressivo: an interpretation

## CZERNY'S SUGGESTIONS FOR PERFORMANCE

Bar 1   Make an 'imperceptible' ritardando on the last three quavers.

Bar 2   Play the last chord 'somewhat ritenuto'.

Bar 4   Play the last three quavers 'with somewhat more fire' and 'almost accelerando'.

Bar 5   'Relinquish' the time again in the last three quavers.

Bar 6   The right hand ornament 'obliges us to employ a ritardando in both hands'. Only the last three notes, though, should be 'perceptibly' retarded. On the last G sharp there should be 'a kind of short pause'.

Bar 9   Play with 'power and spirit', and thus 'almost accelerando'.

Bar 10   Play the second half 'somewhat tranquil'.

Bar 11   The last dissonant chord should be 'soft and somewhat slower'.

Bar 12   The last five quavers form 'a transition into the theme'; there should be a ritardando.

Bar 14   The first crotchet should be played 'somewhat ritardando', holding the pause for 'about' five quavers. The following run must be 'equal, tender and diminuendo', and a marked ritardando should take place on the last 8 notes.

Bar 15   The last ornament is to be played 'with extreme tenderness', and the second half of the bar 'ritardando'.

Bar 15   All the nuances should be intensified when the repeats are played.

Obviously, the extent to which such rhythmic nuances will colour a performance of a Beethoven sonata will depend very much on individual taste. Of all the variable factors that go to make up a performance, this surely is the most uniquely personal one. Czerny, for instance, recommended both a crescendo and an accelerando in the first movement of the 'Moonlight' Sonata, in bars 32–5, the speed and dynamics being reversed in 36–9.[29] In Czerny's advice to performers of the piano sonatas, two points particularly stand out: a response to the 'poetic' qualities of the slow movements, but at the same time a concern that the flow of the music should not be impeded by 'dragging'; his commentary on the first movement ('Andante con Variazioni') of the Op. 26 Sonata in A flat is a case in point:

> In the performance of this theme, the whole art of sustained, harmonious *legato*, and of fine touch, must be called forth, in order to worthily display the noble, and almost religious character of the same. Also it must not be rendered dragging by a too frequent use of the *ritardando*.

There can be no doubt that Beethoven's own playing changed considerably with the onset of deafness.[30] Early reports suggest that it was considered quite the equal of the best, though unique. A notice of a concert at Mergentheim of 1791 observed that Beethoven's playing was 'save for dexterity, more eloquent, imposing and expressive' than any that the writer had heard. 'In a word [the critic added], it touches the heart more'.

As a piano teacher, young Beethoven insisted that 'the motions of both hands and body should be quiet and measured'; and, as we have seen, he based his teaching on C. P. E. Bach's *Versuch*. Yet Cramer was already reporting in 1800 'a certain roughness' in his playing, as well as 'a disturbing uncertainty in the interpretation of one and the same composition – today spirited and full of characteristic expression, tomorrow eccentric even to the point of indistinctness'. Clementi, who heard him seven years later, found that 'his playing was but little cultivated, not seldom violent, like himself, but always full of spirit'. Czerny, possibly the most reliable of the many witnesses simply because he had known Beethoven in his prime, reported that Beethoven played 'fairly strictly' in time. Another pupil, the virtuoso Ferdinand Ries, agreed with Czerny, adding that Beethoven nonetheless played his own compositions 'most eccentrically', now and again making a ritardando during a crescendo 'with fine effect'. Anton Schindler, who only knew Beethoven after the composer had become seriously deaf, described his playing as 'free of all constraint in respect of the beat, for the spirit of his music required that freedom'. Schindler's criticism of Czerny's playing as hard and mechanical, then, needs to be seen in its proper context![31]

Of all Beethoven's contemporaries, Czerny may perhaps be allowed the last word, for he expresses in his 'Concluding remarks' (Op. 500, vol. 4, p. 118) a very proper awareness of the role of the interpreter in the process of musical communication. The search for 'authenticity' can only be the search for boundaries within which the act of 'interpretation' can take place: each great performance, he realises, will be a unique experience:

*Concluding Remarks: On the Intellectual Conception of Beethoven's Works*

If several good actors had to represent the same character (as, for instance, *Hamlet*) each would mostly differ from another in his conception of it, in many of the details. Thus, one would chiefly characterise melancholy, another irony, a third dissembled madness, etc.: and yet each of these representations may be perfectly satisfactory in its way, provided the general view be correct.

So, in the performance of classical compositions, and especially in those of Beethoven, much depends on the individuality of the player (who is presupposed to possess a certain degree of virtuosity; for a stumbler cannot think of intellectual conception). Hence one may principally cause humour to predominate, another earnestness, a third feeling, a fourth bravura, and so on; but he who is able to unite all these, is evidently the most talented.

The higher intellectual conception can only be acquired, even with innate talent, by an intimate acquaintance with *all* Beethoven's compositions, by means of an experienced teacher, and by the observance of all that we have endeavoured to point out, to the best of our ability, in these chapters, and in as minute a manner as the extent of the work has permitted.

POSTSCRIPT: THE PIANO AS ENSEMBLE INSTRUMENT

There is, of course, an extensive repertory of classical chamber music in which the piano has an indispensable part. Indeed, the original titles of much of this music might have led the purchaser to suppose that the pianist played the principal role: Haydn's three trios of 1784, for instance, were published as 'Trios for piano with violin and cello accompaniment'; Mozart's splendid sonatas K301–6 were all entitled 'Sonatas for piano with violin accompaniment'. The convention extended well into the nineteenth century and, indeed, Czerny devoted a whole chapter of his *Art of Playing the Ancient and Modern Piano Forte Works* to 'Beethoven's Works for the Pianoforte with Accompaniments for Other Instruments, or for the Orchestra'. Interestingly, Czerny says not a word throughout this extensive chapter about

balance between piano and 'accompanying' instruments, perhaps for the
very good reason that it was never a problem. Even with wire strings, Tourte
bows and twentieth-century techniques of bowing, string players do now
have difficulty in matching the power of the modern concert grand piano. It
is a question of sound quality as much as of dynamic. Hummel drew
attention to the difference between the Viennese and English piano in
ensemble. Although, he said, the English piano was, if anything, the louder
of the two, it made less impact in ensemble because it had a more sustained
and duller tone. The modern Steinway lacks, even more, the percussive
brightness of a Stein or Walther piano: it therefore *dominates* rather than
*penetrates* in ensemble. Probably no satisfactory modern compromise is possible. To be sure, the sustaining pedal may be used with great discretion, and
textures carefully articulated by touch. But the modern instrument must be
played as a *modern* instrument if the performance is not to sound muzzled.
Perhaps, then, this is an area of interpretation in which a return to period
instruments (or rather, to modern copies) is particularly overdue?

# Notes

1 THE SPIRIT OF AUTHENTICITY

1 His *The Interpretation of the Music of the XVII and XVIII Centuries* (London, 1915) proved to be a pioneering work of enormous importance.
2 Wilhelm von Lenz, *The Great Piano Virtuosos of Our Time*, trans. Philip Reder (London, 1971), p. 9.
3 Igor Stravinsky, *Poetics of Music*, trans. A. Knodel and I. Dahl (London, 1947), p. 129.
4 Paul Hindemith, *A Composer's World* (Cambridge, Mass., 1952), p. 132.
5 Arnold Schoenberg, *Style and Idea*, ed. Leonard Stein, trans. Leo Black (London, 1975), p. 320.
6 Olivier Messiaen, *The Technique of my Musical Language* (Paris, 1944), trans. J. Satterfield (Paris, 1956), chap. 2 ('Rhythm').
7 Ralph Vaughan Williams, *Some Thoughts on Beethoven's Choral Symphony with Writings on Other Musical Subjects* (London, 1953), p. 57. For opposing views on the problem of music's 'knowability' see *Authenticity and Early Music: A Symposium*, ed. N. Kenyon (Oxford, 1988), especially Howard Meyer Brown, 'Pedantry or Liberation'; Philip Brett, 'Text, Context, and the Early Music Editor'; Gary Tomlinson, 'The Historian, the Performer, and Authentic Meaning in Music'; and Richard Taruskin, 'The Pastness of the Present and the Presence of the Past'.

2 BACH'S C MAJOR PRELUDE BWV 870 AND 870A

1 Translated by W. J. Mitchell as *Essay on the True Art of Playing Keyboard Instruments* (London, 1949).
2 BWV 870a, MS P 1089 in the Staatsbibliothek Preussischer Kulturbesitz, West Berlin. See Peter Williams (ed.), *Bach, Handel, Scarlatti: Tercentenary Essays* (Cambridge, 1985), pp. 185ff (Peter le Huray and John Butt, 'In Search of Bach the Organist', p. 185; and Mark Lindley, 'Keyboard Technique and Articulation', p. 229); and 'Early Fingering: Some Editing Problems and Some New Readings for J. S. Bach and John Bull', *Early Music*, vol. 17 (1989), p. 60.
3 This is not to deny that some dynamic variation can be produced on the harpsichord by varying the touch, or that the effect of accentuation can be produced on the organ by the fine control of timing and articulation.
4 When a key is depressed, a metal tangent sets the string vibrating; this tangent stays in contact with the string until the key is released. Too hard a pressure on the tangent can stretch the string and thus raise the pitch. Skilled players actually managed to produce an expressive *Bebung*, or vibrato, by varying the finger pressure on the key.
5 Book 1: Prelude in E minor, Fugue in B minor; Book 2: Preludes in C sharp major, D major, D minor, D sharp minor, F major, A flat major and B minor and Fugues in E minor, F major, A minor, B flat major and B flat minor.

6 Bach, *Versuch*, chap. 3, para. 18. The entire chapter, entitled 'Of good performance', is well worth reading.

7 Translated by Edward R. Reilly as *On Playing the Flute* (London, 1966).

8 C. P. E. Bach had something similar to say about rhythm in his chapter 3.

9 Johann Mattheson, *Der vollkommene Capellmeister* (Hamburg, 1739), p. 151. See also Frederick Neumann, 'Mattheson on Performance Practice', in *New Mattheson Studies*, ed. G. J. Buelow and H. J. Marx (Cambridge, 1983).

10 In these abbreviations the first (arabic) number indicates the bar, the small roman number the beat within the bar; left-hand and right-hand parts are identified with LH and RH.

11 Known to theorists of the time as *figurae*; Bach's cousin J. G. Walther, for instance, discussed them in his *Praecepta der musicalischen Composition* (1708), ed. P. Benary (Leipzig, 1955). See Peter Williams, 'Figurae in the keyboard works of Scarlatti, Handel and Bach' in *Tercentenary Essays*, p. 327. For an attempted systematisation of more than 150 figures, see H.–H. Unger, *Die Beziehungen zwischen Musik und Rhetorik im 16.–18. Jahrhundert* (Würzburg, 1941; reprinted 1969). See also G. J. Buelow, 'Rhetoric and Music', in *The New Grove Dictionary of Music and Musicians*, ed. Stanley Sadie (London, 1980), vol. 15, p. 793.

## 3 CORELLI'S VIOLIN SONATA OP. 5 NO. 11

1 See David Boyden's indispensable *The History of Violin Playing from its Origins to 1761* (London, 1965), especially chaps. 9 and 12. A recording that goes with the book contains comparisons of old and modern instruments and techniques. See also Robin Stowell, *Violin Technique and Performance Practice in the Late Eighteenth and Early Nineteenth Centuries* (Cambridge, 1985), p. 270.

2 Oliver Strunk, *Source Readings in Music History* (New York, 1950), p. 451ff gives extracts. Summaries of the 1689 and 1701 instructions are provided by Kenneth Cooper and Julius Zsako in 'Georg Muffat's Observations on the Lully Style of Performance', *Musical Quarterly*, vol. 53 (1967), p. 220.

3 Strunk, *Source Readings*, p. 486.

4 Published inexpensively in the *Archivum Musicum* series (Florence, 1979), vol. 21.

5 See G. J. Buelow, 'The "Loci Topici" and Affect in late baroque Music', *The Music Review*, vol. 27 (1966), p. 161.

6 See Rosamund E. M. Harding's *Origins of Musical Time and Expression* (London, 1938), chap. 2; Quantz, *Versuch einer Anweisung*, paras. 46–58, and Charles Avison, *An Essay on Musical Expression* (London, 1752).

7 See Walter Kolneder, *Performance Practices in Vivaldi* (Leipzig, 1955), trans. A. de Dadelsen (Winterthur, 1979), p. 19.

8 See Robert L. Marshall, *The Compositional Process of J. S. Bach* (Princeton, 1972), p. 268, for a discussion of Bach's use of Italian terms.

9 See I. Herrmann-Bengen, *Tempobezeichnungen: Ursprung: Wandel im 17. und 18. Jahrhunderts* (Tutzing, 1959), Tabelle III following p. 210.

10 See Kolneder, *Performance Practices*; Robert L. Marshall, 'Tempo and Dynamic Indications in Bach Sources', in *Tercentenary Essays*, p. 259; and David Boyden, 'Dynamics in Seventeenth- and Eighteenth-Century Music', in *Essays on Music in Honour of Archibald Thompson Davison* (Cambridge, Mass., 1957), p. 185.

11 Quoted in Rosamond E. M. Harding, *The Piano-Forte* (Cambridge, 1933), p. 5.

12 Walther, *Musikalisches Lexicon* (Leipzig, 1732; reprinted 1953). See also Sebastian de Brossard's *Dictionnaire de musique* (Paris, 1703; reprinted 1964) and J. Grassineau's *A Musical Dictionary* (London, 1740; reprinted 1966).

13 Marshall (*The Compositional Process*, n. 14, p. 264) suggests, however, that the almost total absence of all dynamics in Bach's solo compositions may reflect 'at least to some significant degree [Bach's] desire to grant the solo performer maximum artistic flexibility in this respect'. He refers here to the solo music for strings, wind, harpsichord, clavichord and organ.

14 Charles Avison, *An Essay*, p. 81.

15 *XII Sonata's or solo's for a Violin, a bass Violin or Harpsichord compos'd by Arcangelo Corelli, his fifth opera, this edition has the advantage of haveing the graces to all the adagio's and other places where the author thought proper by Arcangelo Corelli* (London, 1711). This edition is reproduced in the *Archivum Musicum* (Florence, 1979), ed. Marcello Castellani. See also *Anthology of Music Series* (Cologne, 1949–), vols. 12 (*Improvisation in Nine Centuries of Western Music*, ed. E. Ferand, 1961, p. 112) and 41 (*Original Vocal Improvisations from the Sixteenth to the Eighteenth Centuries*, ed. H. C. Wolff, trans. A. C. Howie, *c.* 1972, pp. 101–32); and B. B. Mather (ed.), *Free Ornamentation in Woodwind Music* (New York, 1976).

16 David Boyden, 'Corelli's Violin Solos Graced by Dubourg', in *Festskrift Hans Peter Larsen* (Copenhagen, 1972), p. 113.

## 4 COUPERIN'S *HUITIÈME ORDRE*

1 François Couperin, *L'art de toucher le clavecin* (2nd edn Paris, 1717), ed. Anna Linde (Wiesbaden, 1933; reprinted 1961).

2 Ibid., p. 41.

3 For a survey of the background see Frederick Neumann, 'The French *Inégales*, Quantz and Bach', *Journal of the American Musicological Society*, vol. 18 (1965), p. 313.

4 See 'Petite dissertation, sur la manière de doigter ...' (*L'art de toucher*).

5 Fifteen French keyboard publications between 1665 and 1750 contain such tables of ornaments; these are reproduced in Paul Brunold, *Traité des signes et agréments employés par les clavecinistes français des XVII & XVIII siècles* (Nice, 1925).

6 Frederick Neumann, *Ornamentation in Baroque and Post-Baroque Music* (Princeton, 1978).

7 Couperin, preface to the *Pièces de clavecin: troisième livre* (Paris, 1722).

8 Henri d'Anglebert, *Pièces de clavecin* (Paris, 1689), and Georg Muffat, *Florilegium Secundum* (Passau, 1698).

9 For further discussion see Frederick Neumann, 'The Dotted Note and the So-Called French Style', *Early Music*, vol. 5 (1977), p. 310; see also below, chap. 5, n. 2.

10 See S. Newman and P. Williams, *The Russell Collection and Other Early Keyboard Instruments in St. Cecilia's Hall, Edinburgh* (Edinburgh, 1968). Recordings from the collection are available from that address.

11 See Ralph Kirkpatrick, *Domenico Scarlatti* (Princeton, 1953), chap. 9.

## 5 BACH'S *OUVERTURE* IN D BWV 1068

1 See Frederick Neumann, 'Once More the "French Overture Style"', *Early Music*, vol. 7 (1979), p. 45.

2 See Frederick Neumann, 'The Question of Rhythm in the Two Versions of BWV 831', in *Studies in Renaissance and Baroque Music in Honor of Arthur Mendel* (Cassel, 1974), p. 183; 'The Dotted Note', p. 310; and 'Once more', p. 39. For contrary views, see John O'Donnell, 'The French Style and the Overtures of Bach', *Early Music*, vol. 5 (1977), pp. 190 and 336; and M. Collins, 'A Reconsideration of French Overdotting', *Music and Letters*, vol. 50 (1969), p. 111.

3 See Arthur Hutchings, *The Baroque Concerto* (London, 1961), especially chaps. 5–6.

4 Joshua Rifkin has, however, persuasively argued for a 'one to a part' performance, throughout: see his recording, on Nonesuch 79036.

## 6 HANDEL'S *MESSIAH*

1 For string techniques, see p. 26; for tempi and dynamics, see p. 36; for instrumentation and orchestral groupings, see pp. 80 and 151; for *notes inégales* and overdotting, see pp. 46 and 72; for additional discussion of ornamentation and articulation, see p. 41 and 58.

2 See Winton Dean, *Handel's Dramatic Oratorios and Masques* (London, 1959), especially chap. 6; Watkins Shaw, *The Story of Handel's Messiah* (London, 1963), and *A Textual and Historical Companion to Handel's Messiah* (London, 1965); and Jens Peter Larsen, *Handel's Messiah: Origins, Composition, Sources* (London, 1957; rev. 1972).

3 See P. G. le Huray, *Music and the Reformation in England* (Cambridge, 1978), pp. 119.

4 Facsimile reprint (London, 1905).

5 His remarks are applicable to all voices, although he mentions only the soprano here.

6 One of Scheibe's main criticisms of J. S. Bach was that he effectively wrote out all the ornaments that the singers were to perform.

7 'Let him learn the manner to glide with the vowels, and to drag the voice gently from the high to the lower notes...' (chap. 1, para. 33).

8 From Handel's *Ottone*: see H. C. Wolff, *Original Vocal Improvisations*, pp. 101–32.

9 Trans. Austin B. Caswell as *A Commentary upon the Art of Proper Singing* (New York, 1968).

10 See Watkins Shaw, *A Textual Companion*, chap. 2, especially p. 70–1; and Donald Burrows, 'Handel's Performances of "Messiah": the Evidence of the Conducting Score', *Music and Letters*, vol. 56 (1975), p. 319; 'The Autographs and Early Copies of "Messiah" ', *Music and Letters*, vol. 66 (1985), p. 201, and *Messiah ... an Urtext Edition* (London, 1987).

11 Shaw, *A Textual Companion*, p. 70; see also chap. 5.

12 A facsimile of the autograph was published by the Sacred Harmonic Society (London, 1868); a facsimile of Handel's conducting score was published for the *Royal Musical Association* by the Scholar Press (London, 1974).

13 See especially Johann David Heinichen, *Der General-Bass in der Composition* (Dresden, 1728) – Bach acted as the Leipzig agent for this book; and Johann Mattheson, *Kleine General-Bass-Schule* (Hamburg, 1735) – Mattheson had heard both Bach and Handel and corresponded regularly with Handel. F. T. Arnold's *The Art of Accompaniment from a Thorough-bass as Practised in the 17th and 18th Centuries* (London, 1931; reprinted 1965) provides a truly encyclopaedic survey of contemporary treatises. For a summary of style problems, and for practical examples, see Peter Williams, *Figured Bass Accompaniment* (Edinburgh, 1970); see also David Ledbetter, *Continuo Playing According to Handel* (London, 1989).

14 See Arthur Mendel, 'On the Keyboard Accompaniments to Bach's Leipzig Church Music', *Musical Quarterly*, vol. 36 (1950), p. 339.

## 7 BACH'S C MINOR PASSACAGLIA BWV 582

1 Of the many studies that have recently been published on organ history and design, the following are particularly helpful: Peter Williams, *A New History of The Organ* (London, 1980), and *The Organ Music of J. S. Bach* (three vols., Cambridge, 1980–4), especially vol. 3; and Fenner Douglas, *The Language of the Classical French Organ* (New Haven, 1967), notably the registration charts on pp. 115–25 and Appendix C, 'Instructions for registration'. See also W. L. Sumner's pioneering work, *The Organ* (London, 1952; fourth edn 1973).

2 See, for instance, Le Bègue's preface to his *Les pièces d'orgue* (Paris, 1676).

3 See Raison, 'Au lecteur', from the *Livre d'orgue* (Paris, 1688).

4 See Williams, *The Organ Music*, vol. 3, p. 52, for an account of Bach as recitalist.

5 See Kerala J. Snyder, 'Buxtehude's Organs (2): The Lübeck Organs', *The Musical Times*, vol. 136 (July, 1985), p. 427.

6 For a concise account of the 'Bach organ', see Williams, *A New History*, chap. 114; a particularly comprehensive discussion is in Williams, *The Organ Music*, vol. 3, pp. 117–90 ('The Music and Its Organ').

7 Peter Williams summarises the source background in *The Organ Music*, vol. 1 (1980), p. 253. All references are to the text of the *Neue Bach-Ausgabe*, IV/7 (Kassel, 1984).

8 For further discussion of texture as articulation, see le Huray and Butt, 'In search of Bach the Organist', p. 185.

9 See Peter le Huray, 'Bach: Phrasing and Articulation', *Organists' Review*, vol. 58 (July, 1973), p. 16.

10 Though Bach probably had no direct hand in the *Schübler* transcriptions (see John Butt, *Bach Interpretation* (Cambridge, 1990), p. 143.

11 See Peter le Huray, 'Phrasing and Articulation', p. 16.

12 The opening variations are given in the *Neue Bach-Ausgabe*, IV/7, p. 148.

13 See Williams, *The Organ Music*, vol. 3, chap. 18, p. 154.

14 See James Dalton, 'Bach Interpretation', *The Musical Times*, vol. 107 (1966), pp. 341, 440 and 536ff.

8  MOZART'S D MINOR STRING QUARTET K421: A CONTEMPORARY ANALYSIS

1  *Versuch einer gründlichen Violinschule* (Augsburg, 1756) Section XII, para. 7. Translated by E. Knocker as *Treatise on the Fundamental Principles of Violin Playing* (London, 1948; rev. 1951).

2  See Peter le Huray and James Day, *Music and Aesthetics in the Eighteenth and Early Nineteenth Centuries* (Cambridge, 1981), p. 286; and Strunk, *Source Readings*, pp. 775 and 782; see also Ian Bent, *Readings in Nineteenth-Century Musical Analysis* (Cambridge University Press, forthcoming).

3  See Albert Palm, 'Momigny', in *Die Musik in Geschichte und Gegenwart*, Cassel, 1961, vol. 9, p. 448.

4  Even if somewhat inaccurately!

9  LEOPOLD MOZART AND THE K421 STRING QUARTET

1  *The Letters of Mozart and his Family*, ed. A. Hyatt King and Monica Carolan, trans. E. Anderson (London, 1966).

2  L. Mozart, *Violinschule* (second edn 1959; rev. 1967). Other substantial violin tutors were soon to follow Mozart's, but none has quite the same relationship to the Viennese 'classical' style (see Stowell, *Violin Technique*).

3  For other extended slurs see, for instance, the first movement of the Piano Concerto in B flat, K595, bars 109–12 and 123–6. See, too, the minuet of the 'Jupiter' Symphony, and the opening movement of the K570 Piano Sonata, bars 101–18. The first edition of the latter joins four separately phrased bars of the first subject (bars 1–4) into one. See also Example 83/2 on p. 127.

4  See Eva and Paul Badura-Skoda, *Interpreting Mozart at the Keyboard*, trans. Leo Black (London, 1962). Despite its age and modest title, this stimulating book is essential reading, covering interpretative problems in almost every kind of music that Mozart wrote; see also Jean-Pierre Marty, *The Tempo Indications of Mozart* (Yale, *c*. 1988).

5  See also L. Mozart, *Violinschule* VII/1/1 and XII/3.

6  For further discussion see Badura-Skoda, *Interpreting Mozart*, chap. 5.

7  In their respective piano tutors of 1828 and 1839 neither Hummel nor Czerny distinguished between dots and dashes.

8  A facsimile of Mozart's autograph is published by the Robert Owen Lehmann Foundation (New York, 1969).

9  Werckmeister, *Harmonologia Musica* (Frankfurt, 1702).

10  Geminiani, *The Art of Playing on the Violin*, op. 9 (London, 1751; ed. David Boyden, London, 1952), p. 8.

11  Though complex enough for a substantial and important study (see Frederick Neumann, *Ornamentation and Improvisation in Mozart* (Princeton, 1986).

10  HAYDN'S 'DRUM ROLL' SYMPHONY IN E FLAT NO. 103

1  See N. Zaslaw, 'Towards the Revival of the Classical Orchestra', *Proceedings of the Royal Musical Association*, vol. 103 (1976–7), p. 158.

2  From Francesco Galeazzi, *Elementi teorico-pratici di musica* (Rome, 1791). Galeazzi was familiar with the famous Mannheim orchestra, and with Italian opera orchestras. The proportions are similar to those suggested by Quantz, whose largest string group is 6,6,3,4,2. It was common 18th-century practice to equate the numbers of first and second violins.

3  Notably, Malcolm Bilson's Mozart piano concerto series on *Archiv*.

4  See Stowell, *Violin Technique*, p. 178.

5  Useful modern studies include Philip Bate, *The Flute* (London, 1969), *The Oboe* (London, 1956), *The Clarinet* (3rd edn rev. F. G. Rendall, London, 1971); Lyndesay G. Langwill, *The Bassoon and Contrabassoon* (London, 1956); R. Morley-Pegge, *The French Horn* (London, 1960); Horace Fitzpatrick, *The Horn and Horn Playing* (London, 1970); and James Blades, *Percussion Instruments and their History* (London, 1970; 2nd edn 1975). See also Anthony Baines, *Woodwind Instruments and their History* (London, 1967), and *Brass Instruments* (London, 1976).

6 Such as those by 'L'Estro Armonico' on *CBS Masterworks* and Brüggen on Philips 422 240-2.

7 Translated by D. Lasocki as *Principles of the Flute, Recorder and Oboe* (London, 1968). For a comprehensive discussion of tonguing, see Anthony Rowland-Jones, *Interpretation and Technique in Playing Recorder Sonatas* (Oxford, 1991), chap. 5. There is also much useful information on fingering and intonation in chaps. 6 and 7.

8 For further details and references, see Mark Lindley, 'Pitch', in *New Grove*, vol. 14.

9 For a challenging discussion of the issues, see James Webster, 'Haydn's Quartet Autographs and Performance Practice', *Isham Library Papers* III (Harvard, 1980), pp. 62ff.

10 *RL*, incidentally, reads the marks as dots, *HU* as dashes.

11 Compare, too, the way in which the timpani articulation of bars 152-3 is treated in the two editions.

12 Momigny, *Cours complet d'harmonie et de composition* (Paris, 1803-6), chap. 46, pp. 583ff.

11 BEETHOVEN'S 'MOONLIGHT' SONATA AND LATE EIGHTEENTH-CENTURY PIANISM

1 Taken from Carl Parrish, 'Criticisms of the Piano When It Was New', *Musical Quarterly*, vol. 30 (1944), p. 428; and Howard Schott, 'From Harpsichord to Pianoforte', *Early Music*, vol. 13 (1985), p. 28. It should be remembered that from the early eighteenth century the term 'cembalo' could refer to the piano, especially if the source were Italian.

2 William S. Newman's *Performance Practices in Beethoven's Piano Sonatas* (New York, 1971; London, 1972) is essential reading.

3 Johann Nepomuk Hummel, *Ausführliche, theoretische-practische Anweisung zum Piano-forte Spiele* (Vienna, 1828), translated (anon.) as *A Complete Theoretical and Practical Course of Instructions on the Art of Playing the Pianoforte* (London, 1828). See part III, sect. II, chap. 4, paras. 3-4.

4 Andreas Streicher, *Brief Remarks on the Playing, Tuning and Care of Fortepianos* (Vienna, 1801), chap. 2, translated by Preethi de Silva in *Early Music Facsimiles* (New York, 1983; second edn., 1988 with facsimile of the German text).

5 Apart, that is, from those in the Finale of Haydn's E flat Sonata, H XVI:52, bar 20.

6 See especially C. P. E. Bach's six extensively fingered keyboard sonatas from the *Versuch*, W. 63, 1-6, ed. E. Doflein (Bonn, 1935).

7 From Czerny's memoirs, quoted in William Sumner, *The Pianoforte* (London, 1966), p. 152.

8 Glyn Jenkins, 'The Legato Touch and the "Ordinary" Manner of Keyboard Playing from 1750-1850' (Ph.D Dissertation, Cambridge, 1976).

9 Türk, *Clavierschule* (Leipzig, 1789), translated and abridged by Dr Callcott as *The Clavier School* (London, 1803; rev. 1975). There is an especially clear discussion of legato touch in vol. 1 of Czerny, *Complete Theoretical and Practical Pianoforte School*, Op. 500 (London, 1839): lesson 18, p. 186 ('On the Legato and Staccato').

10 See David Rowland, 'Early Pianoforte Pedalling', *Early Music*, vol. 13.

11 Kalkbrenner, *Méthode pour apprendre le piano-forte . . . Op.* 108 (Paris, [1830]); translated as *Complete Course of Instructions for the Pianoforte* (London, *c.* 1835); Hummel, *Ausführliche, theoretische-practische Anweisung*, part III, sect. II, chap. 3, para. 3.

12 Czerny, Op. 500 Supplement, chap. 1, p. 6.

13 See Alan Tyson, *The Authentic Editions of Beethoven* (London, 1963), chap. 4, p. 30.

14 Op. 500, vol. 4, chap. 2, p. 32. The second and third chapters, which deal with Beethoven's solo and ensemble piano music, are available in facsimile, entitled *On the Proper Performance of all Beethoven's Works for the Piano* (Vienna, 1970); they include informative commentaries by Paul Badura-Skoda.

15 Anton Felix Schindler, *Beethoven as I Knew Him: a biography* (Münster, 1860), ed. D. W. MacArdle and trans. C. S. Jolly (New York, 1966), p. 415.

16 For a facsimile of the autograph, see the *Viennese Collection of Musical Rareties*, ed. Heinrich Schenker (Vienna, 1921). See also a facsimile of the first edition, published by Walsh, Holmes & Co. (London, 1929). The Universal Urtext edition tends to regard the auto-

graphs (where available) as the principal authority; the Henle Urtext favours the early printed editions; both include original fingerings. A comprehensive source list is in G. Kinsky and H. Holm, *Das Werk Beethovens* (München-Duisburg, 1955); a discussion of the relationship between autographs and editions is in H. Unverricht, *Die Eigenschriften und Originalausgaben von Werken Beethovens* (Kassel, 1960).

17 Lewis Lockwood writes of Beethoven's 'profound concern' over establishing the best possible versions of his works in print – see 'The Autograph of the First Movement of Beethoven's Sonata for Violoncello and Pianoforte, Op. 69', *Music Forum*, vol. 2 (1970), p. 1.

18 For other contemporary evidence, see particularly Friedrich Starke, *Pianoforte-Schule* (three vols., Vienna, 1819–21); and Franz Gerhard Wegeler and Ferdinand Ries, *Biographische Notizen über Beethoven* (Koblenz, 1838). Anton Felix Schindler's *Beethoven as I Knew Him* must be handled with caution.

19 Czerny, *On the Proper Performance*, p. 107.

20 Czerny, *On the Proper Performance*, p. 49.

21 Letter to Karl Holz on the occasion of the publication of the quartet, in *Beethoven's Letters*, ed. E. Anderson (London, 1961), pp. 1241–2.

22 See Stewart Deas, 'Beethoven's "Allegro Assai"', *Music and Letters*, vol. 31 (1950), p. 333.

23 The Scherzo should, however, read dotted minim = 80 (not minim = 80) and the Fugue crotchet (not minim) = 144. Both errors are corrected in the 1819 Artaria edition (see Peter Stadlen, 'Beethoven and the Metronome', *Music and Letters*, vol. 48 (1967), p. 330).

24 The Simrock editions, 'revue, corrigée, métronomisée et doigtée par Charles Czerny' (Bonn, *c.* 1850); see Czerny, *On the Proper Performance* 'Introduction' (p. 1), and 'Commentary' (pp. 1–12), in which Czerny's metronome markings are reproduced.

25 See Nicholas Temperley, 'Tempo and Repeats in the early Nineteenth Century', *Music and Letters*, vol. 47 (1966), p. 323; Peter Stadlen, 'Beethoven and the Metronome', *Music and Letters*, vol. 48 (1967), p. 330; and Michael Tilmouth, 'Repeats', in *New Grove*, p. 746.

26 Cited in Temperley, 'Tempo and Repeats'.

27 Newman, *Performance Practices*, p. 76.

28 Czerny, Op. 500, vol. 3, chap. 3, 'On Occasional Changes in the Time'.

29 *On the Proper Performance*, p. 49.

30 See Franz Kullak, *Beethoven's Piano Playing*, trans. Theodore Baker (London, 1901), p. 7.

31 Schindler, *Beethoven as I Knew Him*, pp. 409–20.

# Contemporary writings on performance practice

Adam, Louis, *Méthode de piano* (Paris, 1804)

Avison, Charles, *An Essay on Musical Expression* (London, 1752)

Bach, C. P. E., *Versuch über die wahre Art das Clavier zu spielen* (Berlin, 1753); trans. W. J. Mitchell, as *Essay on the True Art of Playing Keyboard Instruments* (London, 1949)

Bacilly, Bénigne de, *Remarques curieuses sur l'art de bien chanter* (Paris, 1668); trans. Austin B. Caswell as *A Commentary On the Art of Proper Singing* (New York, 1968)

Bathe, Humphrey, *A Brief Introduction to the Skill of Song* (London, 1597)

Brossard, Sebastian de, *Dictionnaire de musique* (Paris, 1703)

Clementi, Muzio, *Introduction to the Art of Playing on the Piano Forte* (London, 1801)

Couperin, François, *L'Art de toucher le clavecin* (Paris, 1717)

Czerny, Carl, *Royal Pianoforte School* (London, 1839)

Diruta, Girolamo, *Il Transilvano* (Venice, 1593)

Galeazzi, Francesco, *Elementi teorico-pratici di musica* (Rome, 1791)

Geminiani, Francesco, *The Art of Playing on the Violin* (London, 1751)

Grassineau, Jean, *A Musical Dictionary* (London, 1740)

Heinichen, Johann David, *Der General-Bass in der Composition* (Dresden, 1728)

Heinichen, Johann David, *Neu erfundene und gründliche Anweisung* (Hamburg, 1711)

Hotteterre, Jacques, *Principes de la flûte traversière, ou flûte d'Allemagne* (Paris, 1707); trans. David Lasocki as *Principles of the Flute, Recorder and Oboe* (London, 1968)

Hummel, Johann Nepomuk, *Ausführliche, theoretische-practische Anweisung zum Piano-forte Spiele* (Vienna, 1828); trans. anon. as *A Complete Theoretical and Practical Course of Instructions on the Art of Playing the Pianoforte* (London, 1828)

Kalkbrenner, Frederic, *Méthode pour apprendre le piano-forte* ... (Paris [1830]); trans. anon. as *Complete Course of Instructions for the Pianoforte* (London, c. 1835)

Lacépède, H. C. de, *Poétique de la musique* (Paris, 1785)

Lenz, Wilhelm von, *The Great Piano Virtuosos of Our Time*, trans. Philip Reder (London, 1971)

Marpurg, F. W., *Versuch über die musikalische Temperatur* (Breslau, 1776)

Mattheson, Johann, *Kleine General-Bass-Schule* (Hamburg, 1735)

Mattheson, Johann, *Der vollkommene Capellmeister* (Hamburg, 1739)

Milchmeyer, J. C., *Die wahre Art das Pianoforte zu spielen* (Dresden, 1797)

Mozart, Leopold, *Versuch einer gründlichen Violinschule* (Augsburg, 1756); trans. E. Knocker as *Treatise on the Fundamental Principles of Violin Playing* (London, 1948; rev. 1951: 2nd edn 1959)

Momigny, Jerome-Joseph de, *Cours complet d'harmonie et de composition* (Paris, 1803–6)

Muffat, Georg, *Florilegium Primum* (Augsburg, 1695)

Muffat, Georg, *Florilegium Secundum* (Passau, 1698)

Playford, Henry, *Brief Introduction to the Skill of Music* (London, 1664)

Purcell, Henry, *A Choice Collection of Lessons* (London, 1696)

Quantz, Joachim, *Versuch einer Anweisung die Flöte traversière zu spielen* (Berlin, 1752); trans. Edward R. Reilly as *On Playing the Flute* (London, 1966)

Santa Maria, *Arte de tañer fantasia* (Valladolid, 1565)

Schindler, Anton Felix, *Biographie von Ludwig van Beethoven* (Munster, 1840); trans. D. W. MacArdle as *Beethoven as I Knew Him* (New York, 1966)

Streicher, Andreas, *Brief Remarks on the Playing, Tuning and Care of Fortepianos* (Vienna, 1801)

Tosi, Pier Francesco, *Opinioni de cantori antichi e moderni* (Bologna, 1723); trans. as *Observations on the Florid Song* ... (London, 1743)

Türk, Daniel Gottlob, *Clavierschule* (Leipzig, 1789); trans. Dr Callcott as *The Clavier School* (London, 1803)

Walther, J. G. *Musikalisches Lexicon* (Leipzig, 1732)

Walther, J. G., *Praecepta der musikalischen Composition* (Erfurt, 1708)

Werckmeister, Andreas, *Harmonologia Musica* (Frankfurt, 1702)

# Index of musical works cited

# Index of names

# Index of subjects

LIBRARY, UNIVERSITY OF CHESTER

Lightning Source UK Ltd.
Milton Keynes UK
UKOW021126070912

198573UK00003B/2/P